The Cancer Lifeline
Cookbook

Publication of
The Cancer Lifeline Cookbook
was made possible by a grant from

Genentech
BIO ONCOLOGY

Praise for The Cancer Lifeline Cookbook

"Proper nutrition is essential for cancer patients to maintain the quality of their lives and fight their cancer. Cancer Lifeline's new edition of *The Cancer Lifeline Cookbook* is a terrific evidence-based resource of nutritional information as well as specific dietary recommendations to help patients cope with and conquer their disease."

—Albert B. Einstein, Jr., MD
Executive Director, Swedish Cancer Institute, Seattle, WA.

"This is an excellent, thoughtful, and helpful cookbook and guide to healthy eating, both for cancer patients and for healthy individuals wishing to diminish their risk of cancer and cardiovascular disease. The authors provide a thoughtful analysis of current information concerning the role of diet in cancer prevention, and helpful tips concerning management of nausea, diarrhea, and loss of appetite for patients undergoing chemotherapy and radiation therapy."

—Oliver W. Press, MD, PhD
Member, Fred Hutchinson Cancer Research Center; Professor of Medicine and Biological Structure, University of Washington Medical Center, Seattle, WA.

"*The Cancer Lifeline Cookbook* is an excellent resource that is current, concise and informative. The tips to help minimize acute problems are relevant and the basic principles of healthy eating will aid in successful cancer survivorship. I applaud Cancer Lifeline, the authors and many collaborators for creating a book that not only will help patients and families, but will serve as an excellent primer for healthcare professionals."

—Eric Taylor, MD
Radiation Oncology, Virginia Mason Medical Center and Evergreen Hospital Medical Center, Seattle, WA.

"*The Cancer Lifeline Cookbook* is a helpful resource for patients and their caregivers. More than a cookbook, it gathers information about biological interactions that have been shown to affect cancer cells, and how certain foods may increase the body's ability to fight disease and handle side effects from treatment. The recipes are designed to help encourage cancer patients to eat, with intriguing tastes and textures that can keep patients interested in food. The healthy focus is good for the entire family, and is a great direction for the after cancer lifestyle."

—Rick Clarfeld, MD
Surgical Oncology, Northwest Breast Associates, Overlake Medical Clinics, Bellevue, WA.

The Cancer Lifeline | Cookbook

Good nutrition, recipes, and resources to optimize the lives of people living with cancer

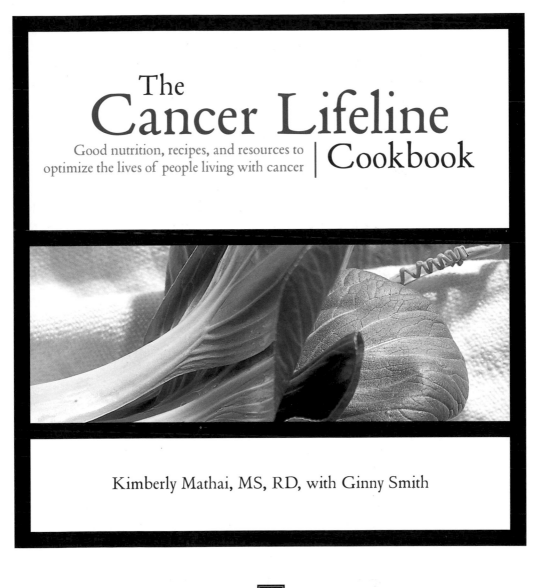

Kimberly Mathai, MS, RD, with Ginny Smith

SASQUATCH BOOKS
SEATTLE

Printed in Singapore by Star Standard Industries Pte Ltd.
Published by Sasquatch Books
Distributed by Publishers Group West
12 11 10 09 08 07 06 05 04   6 5 4 3 2 1

Photographs ©L'Image Magick, Inc./Photography by Diane Padys
Book design: Kate Basart
New American Plate illustration reprinted with permission from the American Institute for Cancer Research.

Library of Congress Cataloging-in-Publication Data
Mathai, Kimberly
        The cancer lifeline cookbook / by Kimberly Mathai with Ginny Smith.
        p.   cm.
        Includes index
        ISBN 1-57061-411-3
        1. Cancer—Diet therapy—Recipes. 2. Cookery for the sick. 3. Cancer—Treatment—Complications—Diet therapy—Recipes. I. Smith, Ginny. II. Title.

        RC271.D52M384 2004
        641.5'631—dc22

                                                                    2003062637

SASQUATCH BOOKS
119 South Main Street, Suite 400 / Seattle, Washington 98104 / 206.467.4300
www.sasquatchbooks.com / custserv@sasquatchbooks.com

Disclaimer

Contents

Dedication

In dedicating this revision, we are compelled to acknowledge Dorothy S. O'Brien and her husband, Bob, caregivers extraordinaire, to whom we are eternally grateful for making our dream of the first edition of *The Cancer Lifeline Cookbook* a reality.

Since its publication, Cancer Lifeline has proudly opened the doors of the Dorothy S. O'Brien Center in Seattle's Green Lake neighborhood. We never imagined that Dorothy and Bob's continued caring and major support of our vision would take us so far.

Thank you, Dorothy and Bob!

We would also like to extend our appreciation to the people at Genentech for underwriting this revision of *The Cancer Lifeline Cookbook* and for having faith in our ability to significantly affect the quality of life for people living with cancer. Thank you for reaching above and beyond our expectations in your efforts to support what we do.

Acknowledgments

Cancer Lifeline owes a large debt of gratitude to the numerous individuals whose personal and professional expertise and insights, long hours of effort, and boundless enthusiasm helped us build upon the success of the first edition of *The Cancer Lifeline Cookbook* and make our cookbook even more valuable as a resource.

At the top of our list are Kimberly Mathai, MS, RD, and Ginny Smith, writer, who devoted month after month to planning, researching, writing, and rewriting the manuscript, and their families, friends, and coworkers who were patient and supportive during those harried times.

We would also like to extend special thanks to Rachel Keim, who authored the original cookbook; all the staff at Cancer Lifeline; Dr. Menghis Bairu, Carol Oshima, and Ken Betzler from Genentech; interns Nikki Gepner, Margo Elbert, Merrilee Buckley, Maribeth Evezich, and David Ingalls, who did everything from contributing recipes to research and analysis; photographer Diane Padys; Patty Wittmann, food stylist; Cynthia Verner, prop stylist; and Gary Luke, Suzanne DeGalan, and all the people at Sasquatch Books. Their professional expertise, talent, enthusiasm, and dedication have played a major role in bringing this book to fruition.

To those who contributed recipes and quality-of-life tips, we are grateful for your insight, experience, and culinary talent. A big thanks goes to Marian Svinth, PhD; Christine Prenovitz, MSW, RYT; Patricia Buschel, RN, MSN, SAAN; horticultural therapist Sheila Taft, HTR; Jenn Steff; Jeanne Ward; Sandi Marcus; Steve Bean; Carolyn Brandon; Clodagh Ash; Jackie Patterson; Marianne Sakamoto; Teresa Woon; Connie Pious; Betty Johanna; Leslie Seeche; Rachel Norton; Linda Peterson; Ann Barry; and Thea Ward; as well as the members of the Cancer Lifeline Support Groups, including the Colorectal Support Group and the Breast Cancer Support Group. Very special thanks also to Sara Snyder, as well as the volunteers at Cancer Lifeline who tested the recipes.

Chefs and restaurants who have contributed recipes to our book include Greg Atkinson, Culinary Consulting; Tom Douglas, Etta's, Palace Kitchen, and Dahlia Lounge; Charles Ramseyer, Ray's Boathouse Cafe; Holly Smith, Cafe Juanita; Kathy Casey; Kaspar Donier, Kaspar's Restaurant and Wine Bar; David deVarona, formerly of Todo Loco Restaurant; Chef Jacques, Metropolitan Market; Jim Watkins, chef/owner of Plenty Fine Foods; Seppo Ed Farrey, author of *3 Bowls: Vegetarian Recipes from an American Zen Buddhist Monastery*; Alvin Binyua, Axis Restaurant; Jean Warren, author of *Super Snacks;* Susan Hodges, author of *Healthy Snacks;* the company chefs at Eden Foods; and interns Margo Elbert and Merrilee Buckley.

In addition, we are grateful to all the individuals who reviewed the manuscript and recipes and offered suggestions. Health care professionals included Rick Clarfeld, MD, Northwest Breast Associates; Dan Labriola, ND, director of the Northwest Natural Health Specialty Care Clinic; Albert B. Einstein, Jr., MD, executive director, Swedish Cancer Institute, Seattle; Oliver W. Press, MD, PhD, Fred Hutchinson Cancer Research Center and University of Washington School of Medicine; David G. Maloney, MD, PhD, Fred Hutchinson Cancer Research Center and University of Washington School of Medicine; Mary Ellen Shands, RN, MN; Jean Stern, MS, RD, CD, Seattle Cancer Care Alliance; Patricia C. Buchsel, RN, MSN, FAAN, Puget Sound Oncology Nursing Society; and Marianne Sterling, RN. Clients, friends, supporters, and Cancer Lifeline staff included Barbara Frederick; Lisa Talbott, MPH; Ellen Zahlis, MN; Michele McNickle; Marianne Svinth, PhD; Pam Tharl; Laura Vanderpool, Parsons Public Relations; David and Marsha Ederer; Sandi Marcus; Dode Capeloto; and Mary Clarfeld.

And finally, we would like to thank all the cancer survivors—as well as their caregivers, family members, and friends—whose desire to make healthy nutritional choices, improve their sense of well-being, and take more control over their lives provided the inspiration for this book in the first place.

Introduction

THE SCIENTIFIC EVIDENCE that diet and lifestyle are linked to cancer is so compelling that the American Cancer Institute estimates that nearly one-third of all cancer deaths are due to these two factors.

In fact, according to cancer experts, if people would eat five or more servings of fruits and vegetables per day, cancer rates would drop by as much as 20 percent.

Nutrition can have a significant impact on preventing cancer and may also have a role in fighting cancer once it has developed. What's more, nutrition and other lifestyle factors may help lower cancer survivors' chances of developing secondary cancers and having recurrences.

Because good nutrition is so important before, during, and after treatment, *The Cancer Lifeline Cookbook* is primarily for people living with cancer and cancer survivors. However, this book is also intended for anyone interested in a health-conscious diet. It sets the stage for a healthier lifestyle from which we all can benefit.

The first edition of our cookbook, which was published in 1996, was created because clients of Cancer

Lifeline kept asking, "So what do I eat now?" Cancer patients are often confused about nutrition because they are encouraged to maintain their weight—even if that means eating a high-fat, high-sugar, low-fiber, low-nutrient diet.

While this may be necessary in some cases, current thinking tells us that it's often possible to maintain weight on a diet that emphasizes healthy fats; quality, protein-rich foods; and high-fiber, nutrient-dense foods. These foods also help boost the body's ability to fight disease.

In developing the second edition of *The Cancer Lifeline Cookbook*, we have updated the scientific information on the link between food and cancer and added a variety of delicious and healthy new recipes. Some of the nation's top chefs have shared their favorite recipes with us to include in the book. We've also added recipes from people in the community, cancer patients, cancer survivors, and people working in the cancer field.

What You Can Expect from
The Cancer Lifeline Cookbook

* Easy-to-understand descriptions of the key components of good nutrition, including the Top 10 "Super Foods," which may protect and fight against cancer.

* Practical, easy-to-implement suggestions for incorporating healthy eating into your lifestyle.

* A variety of recipes for great-tasting, nutritious dishes that are quick and easy to make, even if you're a novice in the kitchen.

* A helpful resource for caregivers who are trying to make meals that are healthy and appetizing for the cancer patient. Many of these caregivers are spouses who have limited cooking experience.

* Suggestions for reducing the side effects of cancer treatment.

* Help in improving your quality of life and your sense of well-being and control.

It is important to remember that diet alone is not the sole cause of any cancer, nor is a nutritious diet alone an effective treatment for cancer. It can be a valuable tool, however, for cancer prevention and treatment.

We hope this book assists you in making choices that feel right for you. Happy reading and healthy eating!

Cancer Lifeline

WE HELP PEOPLE LIVE WITH IT

The warmth of a smile . . . the comfort of a hug . . . the absence of judgment . . . the support of a listening ear . . . the healing of laughter.

That's the essence of Cancer Lifeline. We're a non-profit organization providing cancer patients and their family members, caregivers, friends, and coworkers with the education, resources, and emotional support to live with cancer.

In this spirit of community, Cancer Lifeline was founded in 1973 by a cancer survivor and a group of her close friends who began a 24-hour telephone "Lifeline." We served about 250 people that first year. Since then, our services have grown beyond our wildest dreams.

At our warm, welcoming facility, the Dorothy S. O'Brien Center, our clients can choose classes ranging from exercise, yoga, and meditation to writing, painting, nutrition, and horticultural therapy. In addition to our programs, we offer educational and support groups—including a kids' group and cancer-specific groups—that help families and patients communicate more effectively. Our four Healing Gardens provide a place for clients to rest and reflect. Through our workplace programs, we help managers and coworkers address issues that cancer creates on the job. We now serve about 10,000 people each year, and all of our services except the workplace programs are provided free of charge.

In 1996, we published the first edition of *The Cancer Lifeline Cookbook* in an effort to empower cancer patients, caregivers, and others to actively participate in creating a healthful nutrition plan. This new edition updates and revises that popular book.

We've designed this book to give you a wealth of information and ideas about cooking and eating. We invite you to choose from it whatever makes sense to you on your healing journey.

FOR MORE INFORMATION ABOUT CANCER LIFELINE...

If you'd like to talk to a caring, trained volunteer on our 24-hour Lifeline, call 206-297-2500 if you live in the Seattle area. If you're located outside the Seattle area, dial 1-800-255-5505. Our volunteers offer support, information, and a listening ear.

We also invite you to visit our website at www.cancerlifeline.org. Or you may call our business office at 206-297-2100.

Cancer Lifeline . . .
Optimizing the quality
of life for all people
living with cancer

The Top 10 "Super Foods"

IN A LANDMARK STUDY DONE BY THE American Institute for Cancer Research, an international panel of experts reviewed more than 4,500 research studies to determine the relationship between food, nutrition, and cancer—the second leading cause of death among Americans.

Based on that research, the experts estimated that cancer rates would drop by as much as 20 percent if people would eat five or more servings of fruits and vegetables every day. The panel concluded that vegetables have more scientific support as cancer preventers than fruits, possibly because they have more cancer-inhibiting phytochemicals.

Phytochemicals (*phyto* is a Greek word that means *plant*) are naturally occurring substances that act as natural defense systems in plants, protecting the plants from infections and from the invasion of disease-causing microorganisms. Phytochemicals (also called phytonutrients) provide plants with an abundance of aromas, colors, and flavors.

Foods rich in phytochemicals show potential for reducing the risk of cancer and cardiovascular disease in humans. Phytochemicals in fruits and vegetables have been shown to reduce cancer risk by regulating detoxification enzymes and stimulating the immune system.

Other phytochemicals in foods help ward off heart disease by making blood platelets "slippery" and thus reducing the chance that these cells will get sticky, clump together, and produce clots that may lead to heart attacks.

Phytochemicals work in a number of ways to prevent or suppress cancer. These compounds in plants boost the activities of the body's enzyme systems that detoxify potential cancer-causing substances (carcinogens), block the action of carcinogens on their target organs or tissue, or act on cells to suppress cancer development.

Our list of the Top 10 "Super Foods" represents the best choices of phytochemical-rich foods that are proven to help protect against disease and promote good health. All fruits and vegetables are health-building foods, but current research has shown that some foods are more effective at protecting cells from cancer than others.

Adding the Top 10 foods, as well as a variety of other plant-based foods, to your diet is a great step toward better health, whether you're currently in cancer treatment, a cancer survivor, or just a person who's committed to living a healthier life. Throughout this section you'll find tips for putting the foods to good use, and many of our recipes include these foods as ingredients.

Our Top 10 "Super Foods"

1. Broccoli, cabbage, cauliflower, and other vegetables in the Cruciferous family
2. Beans, including soybeans
3. Berries and cherries
4. Onions, garlic, chives, and other vegetables in the Allium family
5. Carotenoid-rich (deep orange, yellow, red, and green) vegetables
6. Fish
7. Tomatoes
8. Mushrooms
9. Nuts and seeds, including flaxseed
10. Green tea

Note: If you are currently in treatment, some of the Top 10 "Super Foods" may not sound appealing at the moment. That's okay. Just wait and, when you are ready, add them to your meals and snacks.

1 Broccoli, Cabbage, Cauliflower, and Other Vegetables in the Cruciferous Family

POSSIBLE BENEFITS

Vegetables in the cabbage family (called cruciferous vegetables) are rich in cell-protective phytochemicals. These phytochemicals, called indoles, are what give these vegetables their "bite," and they also act to increase liver enzyme activity that's needed to detoxify carcinogens and other foreign compounds.

Foods in the cruciferous family of vegetables also contain another phytochemical compound called sulphoraphane, which encourages the production of certain liver enzymes, possibly helping block tumor growth.

> Cruciferous vegetables include broccoli, Brussels sprouts, cabbage (red, white, napa, and savoy), cauliflower, kale, Swiss chard, parsnips, watercress, radishes, bok choy, collard greens, kohlrabi, rutabaga, turnips, and mustard greens.

Researchers have found that people who eat more broccoli, cabbage, and cauliflower reduce their risk of lung, stomach, colon, rectum, and prostate cancers.

OPTIMIZING CRUCIFEROUS VEGETABLES

Select fresh, organically grown vegetables when they are available. Organic vegetables taste better and greatly reduce the risk of ingesting harmful chemicals. For convenience, keep a supply of frozen cruciferous vegetables like broccoli, cauliflower, or Brussels sprouts on hand.

Some cruciferous vegetables, such as broccoli and cauliflower, are delicious raw or lightly steamed and can be used with dips or added to salads. Other vegetables in this family—such as kale, bok choy, or collards—are best eaten lightly steamed, added to soups, or used in a medley of vegetables for a colorful stir-fry. Try these vegetables in Broccoli with Sesame-Crusted Tofu, page 146, or Garlic-Sautéed Greens, page 139. Peel and dice kohlrabi—a root vegetable that tastes like a mild, sweet turnip—and eat it as a raw vegetable snack, or toss it into a steamed vegetable medley.

If you need to have these vitamin-rich foods very well cooked during treatment, put them in a soup, or purée cooked vegetables in a blender for a creamy, easy-to-digest, and healthful meal.

2 Beans, Including Soybeans

POSSIBLE BENEFITS

Beans are legumes, the technical term for the family of plants that includes pinto beans, black beans, lentils, and soybeans. Beans are rich in such cancer-fighting phytochemicals as saponins, protease inhibitors, and phytic acid.

Saponins are compounds in beans that help keep normal cells from turning into cancer cells and that prevent cancer cells from growing. Other compounds in beans, such as protease inhibitors, protect plants against attacks by viruses and other disease-causing agents.

Cancer researchers have determined that protease inhibitors are extremely potent agents with the ability to suppress the cancer process. Phytic acid, another beneficial compound in beans, may help to enhance immunity and works as an antioxidant to neutralize cell-damaging free radicals.

Beans of all varieties are an outstanding source of fiber, which helps prevent constipation—one of the possible side effects of cancer treatment. They are also excellent sources of protein, calcium, potassium, zinc, and iron.

SOYBEANS AND SOY

The ancient Chinese considered soy, which is native to eastern Asia, to be one of the five sacred grains vital for life. Soy protein is nutritionally equivalent to proteins derived from animal sources, including eggs, milk, and meat. Soybeans and foods from soy include tofu, tempeh, miso, soymilk, soy burgers, and other soy "meats."

Soy foods contain phytoestrogens (weak versions of human estrogen) that act as antioxidants, carcinogen blockers, or tumor suppressors. Isoflavones are one class of these phytoestrogens in soy foods. These substances regulate hormone function in both women and men and may exert a protective effect against hormone-related tumors such as breast and prostate cancer.

Asian populations are known to have a low incidence of breast, prostate, and other cancers. Epidemiologists hypothesize that this may be attributable to the average daily intake of one serving of soy (equal to approximately 40 milligrams of isoflavones).

If you're a breast cancer survivor, you may wonder whether you can safely eat soy, due to its estrogenlike effects. Leading researchers have concluded that it is safe to eat soy in moderate amounts—one to two servings per day—but check with your health care provider for the latest research, just to be sure.

One serving of soy equals
*
1 cup soymilk
$1/2$ cup tofu
$1/2$ cup whole soybeans
$1/2$ cup green soybeans
(edamame)
$1/4$ cup soynuts
$1/2$ cup tempeh
2 tablespoons miso

OPTIMIZING BEANS

Beans make wonderful, inexpensive additions to soups, salads, stews, pasta, and casseroles. Easy, flavorful dips and spreads can be made with garbanzo beans, black beans, or pinto beans (try the Hummus, page 94). Toss beans into your salad, or, for a healthy and fast meal, heat a can of beans with some tomato sauce and seasonings. Have fun experimenting with seasonings and with mixing different kinds of beans. Be adventurous!

If you're just getting friendly with soy foods, try soymilk on your cereal. Soymilk and other soy products are readily available in your grocery store or natural foods supermarket. Grill a soy burger, or add soy sausage or soy breakfast patties to your meals. Marinated or seasoned packaged tofu makes a great addition to stir-fry dishes, or you can slice it and stuff it inside pita bread for a quick grab-and-go meal. Edamame beans—green soybeans—are a tasty, easy-to-prepare side dish; look for the packaged shelled or unshelled beans in the freezer section of the grocery store. Add tofu to the Yogurt Protein Shake, page 72.

In recipes calling for beans, try substituting soybeans for half of the total beans.

Add beans to your diet gradually so your digestive tract has a chance to adjust. The average person can start out by eating half a cup of beans every two or three days, gradually working up to a cup or more per day.

3 Berries and Cherries

POSSIBLE BENEFITS

A variety of berries and cherries contain powerful antioxidant compounds called anthocyanins that protect cells from damage by free radicals. Damaged cells that are not neutralized by antioxidants can replicate and begin the cancer process.

The blue, blue-red, and purple colors in fruits such as blueberries, cherries, grapes, raspberries, and cranberries are produced by anthocyanins. Blueberries, both wild and cultivated, may be one of the richest sources of plant-derived antioxidants.

When scientists tested the antioxidant capacity of berries, the top scorers were blueberries, blackberries, strawberries, and cherries. For example, ½ cup of blueberries equals the antioxidant level of 2½ cups of chopped spinach or 2¼ cups of broccoli florets.

OPTIMIZING BERRIES

Toss fresh or frozen berries into a smoothie, add them to your breakfast cereal, mix some in a fruit salad, or just snack on fresh berries. Fresh, seasonal berries are usually available from May through September. The rest of the year, buy frozen berries. Try our recipe for Simply Delicious Berries, page 214, or Blueberry Breakfast Cake, page 79, for tasty ways to eat your anthocyanins.

4 Onions, Garlic, Chives, and Other Vegetables in the Allium Family

POSSIBLE BENEFITS

Garlic, onions, leeks, shallots, and other vegetables in the *Allium*—or onion—family are rich in sulfur-containing compounds called allyl sulfides. These compounds act as cancer-blocking or cancer-suppressing agents.

Allyl sulfides also work to increase toxin-eliminating enzymes in the liver that sweep cancer-causing chemical substances (procarcinogens) out of the body. These compounds also increase the activity of certain immune system cells, like macrophages and T lymphocytes.

Allium vegetables also contain sulfur compounds called diallyl disulfides (DADS). Garlic is a rich source of this powerful anticancer phytochemical, which works to slow the growth of cancer cells.

OPTIMIZING ALLIUM VEGETABLES

Crush fresh garlic and add it to your salad dressing. Bake a garlic bulb and use the soft cloves as a topping for crusty bread. Add onions to sauces and soups. Chop fresh chives and toss them in your salads. Get your alliums in Grilled and Roasted Walla Walla Sweet Onions with Pine Nut Butter, page 140, or Roasted-Garlic Garlic Bread, page 152.

5 Carotenoid-Rich (Deep Orange, Yellow, Red, and Green) Foods

POSSIBLE BENEFITS

While all produce is good for you, a number of fruits and vegetables contain compounds called carotenoids that may protect against rapid cell production, which can increase the risk of cancer.

Carotenoids are present in deep orange, green, yellow, and red vegetables and fruits. They contain antioxidants, compounds that are important in fighting free radicals—the by-products of the natural activity of oxygen in cells. Free radicals are very reactive and roam the body, damaging cells and the genetic material within them. This can hinder the natural ability of cells to resist the development of cancer.

Our cells have well-developed systems for fighting free radicals and mending the damage they cause, and we can assist the cells by eating an antioxidant-rich diet. Many studies have reported a relationship between low risk for cancer and high consumption of foods containing antioxidants.

OPTIMIZING CAROTENOID-RICH FOODS

Add a rainbow of brightly colored fruits and vegetables to your meals and snacks. In the vegetable family, yams, squash, and sweet potatoes deliver the highest amount of carotenoids actually absorbed by the body. Fruits such as melons, peaches, oranges, and papayas are also excellent sources of carotenoids. Gingered Carrot Soup, page 121, or Baked Sweet Potato Fries, page 135, deliver these nutrients with wonderful flavor.

Eat any of the carotenoid-rich foods as often as you like. Many fresh fruits and vegetables can be washed, cut up, and stored in airtight containers so you'll have plenty of fresh, healthy foods readily accessible for snacks or cooking.

> Carotenoid-rich foods include spinach, sweet potatoes, yams, carrots, squash, bell peppers, cantaloupe, mangoes, peaches, oranges, strawberries, nectarines, papayas, and apricots.

6 Fish

POSSIBLE BENEFITS

Fish is rich in omega-3 fatty acids, a healthy fat that appears to reduce the risk of certain cancers. In one study of people who ate one or more servings of fish a week, there was a reduced risk of gastrointestinal cancers, including colon cancer.

Fish seems to protect against cancer by restricting the production of prostaglandins—inflammatory compounds that act as tumor promoters. Research scientists are studying the effects of a combination of DHA (one of the omega-3 compounds in fish and fish oil) packaged with chemotherapy drugs to target cancer cells without damaging healthy cells.

> Try substituting sweet potatoes in recipes calling for white potatoes.

Eating fish is also good for your heart. The American Heart Association recommends that adults eat at least two servings of fish per week. The fish that are highest in omega-3 fats include mackerel, salmon, sardines, rainbow trout, herring, and albacore tuna. Cod, flounder, clams, catfish, haddock, perch, and halibut have lower amounts of omega-3 fatty acids.

OPTIMIZING FISH

Make a habit of eating fish frequently, poached, baked, or lightly sautéed with some garlic. Go for convenience if your energy resources are limited: purchase canned fish and use it in salads, add it to a sandwich, or just eat it out of the can as a snack. Add the Salmon with Sun-Dried Tomato Sauce, page 170, or Pan-Seared Petrale Sole with Lemon Caper Butter Sauce, page 165, to your menus for a delicious way to eat more fish.

7 Tomatoes

POSSIBLE BENEFITS

Tomatoes contain lycopene, a phytochemical that has several anticancer effects. Lycopene acts as a potent antioxidant to stop free radicals from tearing through the body's cell membranes and harming the DNA. This phytonutrient also helps to restore the normal cellular communication that is lacking in tumors. When the cells are able to communicate, cancer cells can be signaled to halt their growth.

In Mediterranean countries, where people eat a lot of tomatoes as well as other fruits and vegetables, there are lower cancer rates. One study showed that when men ate 10 or more servings of tomato products per week, they experienced a 35 percent reduction in prostate cancer. The effects were even stronger with more advanced or aggressive prostate cancer. Lycopene also appears to be effective against breast cancer.

Processed tomato products such as spaghetti sauce, tomato paste, purée, and juice have two to eight times more lycopene than raw tomatoes. Other red fruits and vegetables that contain lycopene include watermelon, pink grapefruit, apricots, and pink guavas.

OPTIMIZING TOMATOES AND OTHER LYCOPENE-RICH FOODS

Enjoy a rich tomato sauce on your steamed vegetables. Drink tomato juice as a snack. Make a nourishing soup like Basil-Spiked Tomato Soup, page 110, and add a quick and easy mini pizza (top an English muffin with pizza sauce, lightly steamed veggies, and a sprinkle of low-fat cheese). Snack on grapefruit, apricots, or a slice of watermelon.

Mushrooms

POSSIBLE BENEFITS

Mushrooms have been revered in Asia as potent medicines for thousands of years. In fact, Chinese emperors and Japanese royalty drank mushroom teas and concoctions to achieve vitality and long life. Mushrooms are low in calories and carbohydrates and rich in vegetable proteins and essential amino acids. They are a source of some fiber and contain a number of important vitamins and minerals, including B vitamins, iron, potassium, selenium, and zinc.

There is evidence that shiitake and maitake mushrooms also contain polysaccharides, substances that may stimulate the immune system and provide anticancer protection. Polysaccharides may increase the production of immune system defenders such as cytokines and macrophages, which recognize and destroy cancer cells, viruses, and bacteria.

Shiitake mushrooms contain a form of polysaccharide called lentinan, a substance that appears to stimulate the body's own antioxidant defense system and activate the body's immune system. Animals given lentinan derived from shiitake mushrooms developed significantly smaller tumors than those not receiving the lentinan.

The maitake mushroom, also known as hen of the woods or dancing mushroom, contains a polysaccharide compound called beta-glucan or

D-fraction. Beta-glucan appears to increase the action of natural killer (NK) cells, which regulate immune system responses and cause the death of tumor cells.

Studies on the protective qualities of shiitake, maitake, and other mushrooms have used only compounds extracted from mushrooms, so it's unknown whether eating fresh mushrooms in relatively small quantities will provide any protective effects. Nevertheless, mushrooms are a healthy, nutritious food that may have medicinal properties, so enjoy the many delicious and intriguing varieties.

OPTIMIZING MUSHROOMS

Use shiitake or maitake mushrooms in place of more common mushrooms such as button mushrooms. Mushrooms have a wonderful, meaty texture and can be added to stir-fries, soups, or casseroles. Arame Stuffed Mushroom Caps, page 136, or creamy Czech Mushroom Soup, page 114, make an elegant addition to any meal or party. Most stores carry many varieties of mushrooms, including shiitake and maitake.

9 Nuts and Seeds, Including Flaxseed

POSSIBLE BENEFITS

Nuts are nutritional wonders. They provide concentrated energy in small packages and contain large amounts of protein, minerals, and vitamins. Brazil nuts, almonds, cashews, and walnuts contain about 6 grams of protein in ⅓ cup, as well as 1 to 2 grams of fiber.

Nuts and nut butters are excellent choices during cancer treatments, when eating may be a challenge. On the other hand, a small amount of nuts goes a long way: just ⅓ cup has 240 to 300 calories. Nuts are high in fat, but it is mostly unsaturated, a healthy form of fat.

Nuts appear to have a positive effect on prostate cancer. Researchers who studied data on men from 59 countries found that as consumption of nuts and seeds increased, mortality from prostate cancer decreased.

Walnuts have a compound called ellagic acid that inhibits certain carcinogen-induced cancers and may have other cancer-preventing properties. Cancer cells treated with ellagic acid showed slowed overall cell growth and malignant cell death (apoptosis). Walnuts have also been shown to lower cholesterol.

In one study, animals exposed to cancer-causing compounds and fed a diet of whole almonds showed a reduction in cancer-promoting conditions such as rapidly dividing cells.

Flax and flaxseed contain several important health-protective substances, including fiber (more fiber than in oat bran) and alpha-linolenic acid, an omega-3 fatty acid that is linked to a lower risk of heart disease and cancer.

Flaxseed is a rich source of lignans, compounds that are transformed by the bacteria in our bodies into hormone-like substances (phytoestrogens) that may protect against tumor formation and growth.

Researchers have found that flaxseed reduces tumor size and numbers in animals and humans. Estrogen-receptor negative breast cancer patients who ate a daily muffin containing 25 grams of flaxseed for 39 days experienced reduced breast tumor growth. In addition, flaxseed (30 grams a day) and a low-fat diet (20 percent fat) lowered prostate-specific antigens (PSA) levels in prostate cancer patients after an average treatment time of 34 days.

Cautions on Flaxseed
*

If you are a cancer patient with estrogen-receptor positive cancer and are taking drugs like tamoxifen, eat flaxseed in moderation—about 1 tablespoon or 10 grams a day. There are fewer clinical trials to guide us in this area.

Ground flaxseed is a better choice than flaxseed oil if you have prostate cancer. Flaxseed contains lignans that appear to bind to testosterone and decrease circulating levels of this hormone, which is a good thing for prostate cancer. Use about 2 tablespoons of the ground seed daily.

OPTIMIZING NUTS AND FLAXSEED

Sprinkle chopped nuts on cereal, stir them into yogurt, or add some to your favorite salad. Toss nuts into stir-fries, salads, and pasta. Experiment with different types of nuts in your favorite muffin or pancake recipe. Spread almond, peanut, or other nut butters on bread and waffles.

Flaxseed can be purchased as whole seeds, meal, flour, or oil. Grind whole seeds into a meal, using a coffee mill or blender. Sprinkle ground flaxseed on cereal or salads, or mix it into soups. Flaxseed can also be added to muffins, breads, and cookies.

10 Green Tea

POSSIBLE BENEFITS

Both green and black tea, but not herb teas, contain phytochemicals called polyphenols and related compounds. These compounds act as powerful antioxidants and may also limit cell replication, a primary characteristic of cancer.

Polyphenols in tea are known to inhibit compounds that are involved in tumor survival and metastasis. They also thwart the activities of many tumor-associated compounds that drive cell growth.

Compounds in green tea such as polyphenols help eliminate free radicals that can alter DNA, causing cell mutation and leading to cancer formation. One study found that Japanese women who drank three or more cups of green tea daily had a lower recurrence of stage 1 and stage 2 breast cancers after seven years.

Researchers who studied the effect of green tea on prostate cancer found that PSA levels dropped 43 percent in men with prostate cancer who took green tea supplements. (Note: Herb/drug interactions with green tea supplements have been reported. Talk with your doctor, nurse, or nutritionist about possible interactions with your medications.)

OPTIMIZING GREEN TEA

Make green tea your beverage of choice. While black tea contains polyphenols, studies show that the antioxidant compounds in green tea may have more of an effect than those in black tea.

Enjoy a cup of tea with your breakfast, and make your caffeine count: green tea has health benefits with only moderate amounts of caffeine, and even decaffeinated green tea provides the benefits of the phytochemicals. Start your own teatime—have a late-afternoon break with a cup of tea. In the summer, brew iced green tea for a refreshing pick-me-up. Don't drink tea that is too hot; it may increase the risk of esophageal cancer.

Nutrients That Promote Good Health

GETTING ALL THE NUTRIENTS YOUR body needs to run optimally is important for everyone, but it's especially important for cancer survivors. As your body is recovering from disease, it needs all the help it can get to repair and rebuild healthy tissue. Because eating may be more difficult during recovery, it is advantageous to pack as many nutrients as possible into the foods you do eat.

Your body requires six basic nutrients. Water is the nutrient needed in the greatest quantity, followed by protein, carbohydrates, fat, vitamins, and minerals. Protein, carbohydrates, and fat are called macronutrients because your body needs them in large quantities. Vitamins and minerals are called micronutrients because they are needed in smaller amounts.

Water

You may not think of water as one of the key nutrients, but it is. Water makes up approximately 50 to 60 percent of the body's weight. It brings to your body's cells the exact nutrients they need and carries away waste products.

Water helps your body digest food, transport other nutrients, maintain normal body temperature, flush toxins, and remove waste products. Fatigue, a common side effect of cancer treatment, can be exacerbated by not drinking enough fluid. Your body excretes approximately 3 quarts of water every day. To replace that water, drink at least 2 quarts of fluids throughout the day. (You may need more fluids if you're on chemotherapy, or less if your sodium level is out of balance. Your nurse, doctor, or nutritionist can advise you on the amount that's right for you.) You can consume another quart of water simply by eating plenty of fruits and vegetables.

To get your fluid quota, choose water, mineral waters (varieties without added sodium), bottled water flavored with fruit essence (avoid waters with added sugars), or fruit juice diluted with sparkling water. Herbal tea, without caffeine, is also a good choice. Many people like to keep a bottle of water with them at all times to make drinking more convenient.

Limit your consumption of caffeinated sodas, coffee, and alcohol. They may have a dehydrating effect that can rob your body of fluid.

Macronutrients

The macronutrients—protein, fat, and carbohydrates—are the body's primary source of fuel, and they also play a major role in maintaining the balance of many of the hormones and enzymes in the body. Two of those hormones, insulin and glucagon, control the sugar levels in the blood and the enzymes that balance the body's metabolic processes. These metabolic processes produce energy, help regulate your immune system, and control many other body functions.

A diet that provides a healthy balance of macronutrients is especially important if your body has been stressed or compromised by disease and treatment.

PROTEIN: THE BODY'S BUILDING BLOCKS

The body uses protein to build, maintain, and repair tissue. It helps regulate many of the body's chemical processes. Normal protein intake is about 56 grams a day for men, 46 grams for women. However, during cancer treatment your body is under a great deal of stress, so you may need more protein—80 grams or more each day—to repair and rebuild tissue and help prevent infection.

How much protein do you need? Protein needs vary from person to person, and your need will probably fluctuate as you progress through treatment and recovery. Work with a nutritionist or your nurse or doctor to determine your optimal protein intake before, during, and after treatment.

Sources of Protein

Most of the foods we eat contain some protein, but some foods have more protein than others. Here are a few examples.

About 7 grams of protein:

    1 ounce lean meat, poultry, or fish

    ½ cup legumes

    ¼ cup tofu

    1 cup broccoli or Brussels sprouts

    ½ cup cottage cheese

    1 cup egg noodles

    7 ounces milk or yogurt

    1 ounce cheese

    2 tablespoons peanut butter

    1 egg

    1 to 2 ounces nuts or seeds

About 3 grams of protein:

    ⅓ cup cooked rice

    ½ cup cooked cereal or grains

    1 slice of bread

About 2 grams of protein:

    1 cup raw vegetables

    ½ cup cooked vegetables

As you choose protein sources, remember that the goal is to minimize your consumption of animal protein and maximize your consumption of plant-based protein.

Good choices for animal proteins include skinless chicken and turkey, fish and shellfish, lean cuts of red meat (round, loin, or flank), eggs, low-fat and nonfat cheeses, and other nonfat dairy products such as yogurt and milk. Avoid processed meats, organ meats, and fatty cuts of red meat.

Plant proteins—which include beans, nuts and seeds, and some grains—provide quality protein and add variety to your meals. Make liberal use of legumes, grains, and vegetables in your diet. Other excellent sources of plant protein include tofu and other soy products, dried beans, brown rice, barley, and nuts such as almonds and walnuts.

Legumes are the fruit or seeds of leguminous plants. They include kidney beans, soybeans, split peas, lentils, black-eyed peas, and lima beans. Their specially adapted root systems trap nitrogen in the soil and turn it into compounds that become part of the seed. The result? Legumes are richer in high-quality protein than most plant foods.

The notion that plant foods need to be specially combined at each meal to make "complete" protein is outdated. The body pools and stores amino acids from foods in muscle and other tissues and uses them to assemble proteins as needed.

Use These Formulas to Estimate Your Daily Protein Needs
*

FOR NORMAL PROTEIN NEEDS: Normally, you need 0.4 gram of protein per pound of body weight. For example, if you weigh 150 pounds, your protein needs are 0.4 x 150, or about 60 grams of protein per day.

DURING TREATMENT, OR IF YOUR BODY IS UNDER OTHER STRESS, SUCH AS FIGHTING AN INFECTION: Under stress, your body's needs increase to 0.7 to 0.8 gram of protein per pound of body weight. For example, if you weigh 150 pounds, your protein needs are 0.7 x 150, or about 105 grams of protein per day.

Experiment with creating meals that emphasize plant proteins. Some winning combinations include:

* Beans, salsa, and low-fat cheese wrapped in a tortilla
* Bread and peanut butter with your favorite add-in (such as a sliced banana)
* Tofu and vegetable stir-fry
* Bean and vegetable soup combined with green salad or crusty bread

CARBOHYDRATES: THE BODY'S PREFERRED FUEL

Carbohydrates are the body's primary source of immediate fuel. They offer a wide variety of nutrients that nourish the brain and central nervous system, provide energy, and help keep your bowel movements regular. Fiber found in whole foods such as fruits, vegetables, beans, and grains stimulates the muscles of the digestive tract so that they retain their health and tone. This in turn speeds up the transit time of materials—including those linked with cancer—through the colon. Fiber also maintains bowel health and may reduce the incidence of colon cancer.

During treatment, some foods, including beans or nuts and seeds, may be harder to digest. You can add these foods back into your menus after your treatment.

Optimal Carbohydrates are whole foods and minimally processed foods that contain all their fiber and vitamins. They have many components, so it takes time for them to be broken down and reach your bloodstream. They make the best all-around fuel because they "burn" slowly and can help increase your feelings of stamina.

Highly Processed Carbohydrates, on the other hand, have had their fiber and vitamins removed and are digested and absorbed into the bloodstream more quickly. They don't provide the feelings of stamina and endurance that complex carbohydrates do. In fact, they promote greater increases in blood sugar and insulin levels, which can lead to increased fatigue.

Sources of Carbohydrates

The best sources of optimal carbohydrates are dried beans and peas; unprocessed grains such as brown rice, polenta, and quinoa; whole-grain bread, whole-grain cereals, and pasta; and fruits and vegetables.

Limit your intake of highly processed carbohydrates such as baked goods that contain a lot of sugar, sweetened cereals made from white flour rather than whole grains, candy, and soda. Try to use less white rice and pasta made from white flours.

FAT: MAKING THE BEST CHOICES

The body is constantly using small amounts of fat for fuel. Fat in moderate amounts is essential for good health, but most people eat too much of the wrong kind of fat. Although all types of fat have similar amounts of calories, there is some evidence that certain types, such as saturated fats, may increase cancer risk.

Types of Fat

Saturated fat comes from tropical oils such as coconut milk and palm oil and from animal sources such as butter, meat, lard, and whole-milk products. It is usually solid at room temperature. This type of fat raises blood cholesterol and increases the risk of heart disease. High cholesterol may also be linked to an increased risk of lung and pancreatic cancer.

Polyunsaturated fat comes from plant sources, such as corn, soy, and safflower oils, and is liquid at room temperature. These fats occur in food as either omega-3 or omega-6 fatty acids. Omega-6 polyunsaturated fats are the oils used most by the food and restaurant industry. These oils may help to lower cholesterol, and they do not appear to promote cancer.

Omega-3 fatty acids are highly polyunsaturated fats found in fish such as salmon and mackerel as well as in leafy vegetables and flaxseed and flax oil. These fatty acids have an anticlotting action that may be effective in preventing heart attack and stroke. They may also improve immune function and, in animal studies, have been shown to inhibit tumor growth.

The recommended intake of omega-3 fatty acids is 1.6 grams a day for men and 1.1 grams a day for women. There are 1.5 grams of omega-3 fats in 6 ounces of cooked (8 ounces of raw) salmon or rainbow trout or in 3 ounces of canned sardines. A 6-ounce serving of most other fish—including cod, flounder, tuna, clams, catfish, haddock, perch, and halibut—has between 0.2 and 0.9 gram of omega-3 fats.

Monounsaturated fat comes from plant sources and includes olive, canola, peanut, sesame, avocado, and walnut oils. Nuts and seeds, such as walnuts and pumpkin seeds, fall into this category. Monounsaturated fat, which is liquid at room temperature, reduces only the damaging LDL cholesterol and leaves HDL cholesterol untouched. (LDL cholesterol promotes heart disease but HDL cholesterol protects against heart attacks.)

People in Greece and Italy who consume a lot of monounsaturated fat tend to have less heart disease and cancer, even though they have fairly high-fat diets. Since most people eat more omega-6 fats than omega-3 fats, using more monunsaturated fats like canola oil, olive oil, or nuts and seeds can help bring you back to a good balance of omega-6 to omega-3.

Hydrogenated Fat (also called *trans fat*) is a polyunsaturated fat that has been chemically changed. In the transformation process, hydrogenated fat loses its unsaturated character and the health benefits that go with it. Hydrogenated and partially hydrogenated oils are found in commercially prepared baked goods, shortenings, and deep-fried foods. These fats act like saturated fats in the body and should be avoided.

Desirable Sources of Fat

If you're losing weight and are being encouraged to eat more calories in the form of fat, be sure to select fat that has nutrients in it. For example, choose the following:

✷ Milkshakes made with soymilk, yogurt, or tofu instead of with ice cream (see our Yogurt Protein Shake, page 72)

✷ Peanut butter or almond butter, instead of butter, spread on bread or waffles

✷ Avocado instead of mayonnaise in a sandwich or on toast

✷ Fatty fish such as salmon instead of white fish or red meat

To cut back on fat, begin choosing low-fat or nonfat milk products; lean broiled, baked, or braised meats; skinless fish or poultry; and fresh fruits and vegetables prepared without oils or cream. Try getting more of your protein from plant sources such as dried peas and beans, tofu, grains, and vegetables.

Micronutrients

While your body needs micronutrients in smaller quantities than it does macronutrients, each of them is essential to achieving and maintaining good health.

VITAMINS: NECESSARY FOR LIFE AND GROWTH

Vitamins are chemical compounds that the body requires in small amounts. While they don't provide energy, they help the body process and use the energy it gets from food. Most vitamins cannot be made by the body or are not made in sufficient quantities to meet the body's needs, so they must be supplied by food.

Diets rich in foods containing antioxidant vitamins—E, C, and beta-carotene (a plant form of vitamin A)—may protect against many forms of cancer, including oral, esophageal, and reproductive-system cancers. Many studies have linked consumption of foods rich in vitamin C with a reduced risk of cancer.

Sources of Vitamins E, C, and Beta-Carotene

Fruits: fruits and juices of citrus, apricots, kiwis, mangoes, peaches, strawberries, cantaloupe and other melons, and papayas

Vegetables: carrots, broccoli, Brussels sprouts, sweet potatoes, red and green peppers, tomatoes, peas, and spinach

MINERALS: THE BODY'S REGULATORS

Minerals are found in all body tissues and fluids. They help the body build tissue, regulate body processes, maintain fluid balance, and use the energy from food. They do not provide energy.

It is essential that we consume enough minerals to ensure the proper functioning of our bodies. For cancer survivors, who may be eating less, it can be difficult to get sufficient quantities of minerals, including potassium, magnesium, calcium, iron, and selenium.

Several studies have suggested that foods high in calcium might help reduce the risk of colorectal cancer, and the relationship of selenium to cancer has been the focus of numerous studies. In one study, researchers found that men with low levels of plasma selenium had a four- to fivefold increased risk of prostate cancer. Studies on animals suggest that selenium protects against cancer, especially lung, colon, and prostate cancer.

Treatment and its side effects can result in deficiencies in essential minerals, so try to pack your diet with whole foods—fruits, vegetables, beans, and grains—that can help your body replace them.

Sources of Minerals (listed from highest to lowest)

Calcium: collard greens (1 cup, cooked), calcium-fortified orange juice (1 cup), sardines (3 ounces, canned), soymilk (1 cup), cow's milk (1 cup), sea vegetables (dulse, 3 ounces, dry), figs (10 medium), almonds (¼ cup), tofu (½ cup), navy beans (1 cup, cooked), broccoli (1 cup, cooked).

Iron: tofu (½ cup, firm), baked beans (1 cup), blackstrap molasses (1 tablespoon), spaghetti with tomato sauce (1 cup), apricots (10 dried halves), spinach (1 cup fresh), green peas (½ cup, cooked), whole wheat bread (1 slice), roasted chicken breast (1), broccoli (½ cup, cooked).

Magnesium: kidney beans (½ cup, cooked), spinach (½ cup, cooked), almonds (1 ounce, 24 nuts), soybeans (½ cup, cooked), pumpkin seeds (1 ounce, 88 seeds), potato (1 medium, baked), beet greens (½ cup, cooked), broccoli (½ cup, cooked), raspberries (1 cup), carrots (½ cup, cooked).

Potassium: dates (6, dried), cantaloupe (½ melon), potato (1 medium, cooked), lima beans (½ cup, cooked), banana (1 medium), spinach (½ cup, cooked), broccoli (1 cup, cooked), salmon (4 ounces, canned), tomato (1 medium), peanuts (1 ounce).

Selenium: Brazil nuts (¼ cup), fish (including snapper, halibut, salmon, scallops, 3 ounces, baked), sunflower seeds (¼ cup), whole wheat bread (1 slice).

Sea Vegetables: A Great Source of Minerals

Sea vegetables contain 10 to 20 times the minerals of land plants. Sea vegetables such as nori, kombu, hijiki, dulse, and wakame are excellent sources of calcium, magnesium, and potassium—and they add minerals while enriching the flavor of foods. Nori, for example, is one of the richest sea-vegetable sources of protein and also contains large amounts of vitamins C, B1, and A.

Adding sea vegetables to your favorite recipes is easy. For dishes that cook longer than an hour, toss in whole or cut-up sea vegetables like kombu or wakame at the beginning of the cooking period. They lend a wonderful rich flavor to dishes, especially stews. For dishes that cook for less than an hour, soak the quicker-cooking sea vegetables—like arame—for 10 minutes, until they are soft enough to cut. Then cut them up and add them to the dish. (Or try our recipe for Arame-Stuffed Mushroom Caps on page 136.) When eating out, vegetarian nori rolls are a great way to enjoy sea vegetables.

> **Boost Iron**
> *
> To enhance the absorption of iron, add vitamin C—rich foods—such as kiwi, broccoli, red bell pepper, papaya, and citrus fruits—to your diet.

Supplements to Your Diet

It's important to get as many of your daily nutrients as possible from vitamin-rich whole foods, such as fruits, vegetables, beans, and grains. This is because some substances contained in whole foods are not available in supplement form. In fact, there may be important substances in food of which we aren't even aware.

Since optimal nutrition is essential when you're fighting disease, taking supplements may be a beneficial choice, especially if you are having difficulty eating. It is believed that good nutrition decreases recovery time, speeds return of the senses of smell and taste to normal, promotes healing of wounds, and helps restore a sense of well-being more quickly.

Talk to your doctor, nurse, or nutritionist before taking supplements if you're in treatment. High doses of supplements may interfere with chemo or radiation therapy.

Creating a Healthier Diet

WE HAVE DISCUSSED THE BENEFITS of eating a primarily plant-based diet using fruits, vegetables, beans, nuts and seeds, and whole grains, including the Top 10 "Super Foods." We've also covered the basic building blocks of nutrition, including fats, carbohydrates, proteins, vitamins, and minerals.

How do we put all these components together to create a healthier diet? Picture your plate with two-thirds plant foods and one-third or less lean meat, poultry, fish, or low-fat dairy products. The American Institute of Cancer Research calls this the New American Plate and recommends that you use it as a model as you begin eating smaller portions of meat and larger portions of vegetables, grains, beans, and other plant foods.

Thinking about your plate in this way will help you achieve your daily goal of eating five to nine servings of a variety of fruits and vegetables.

Getting these servings shouldn't be daunting if you understand portion sizes. Eat any one item listed below and you have eaten the equivalent of one serving.

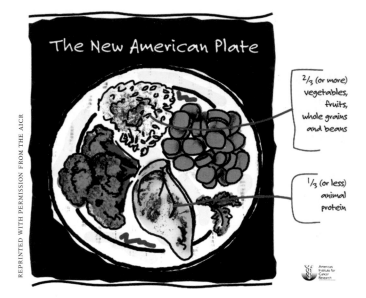

The New American Plate

2/3 (or more) vegetables, fruits, whole grains and beans

1/3 (or less) animal protein

American Institute for Cancer Research

Fruits and Vegetables

Foods that equal one serving:

* 1 medium apple, banana, or orange
* ½ cup chopped cooked or canned fruit
* ¾ cup fruit or vegetable juice
* 1 cup raw leafy vegetables
* ½ cup other vegetables (cooked or raw)

> Grains, dried beans (legumes), root vegetables (beets and parsnips), tubers (potatoes and yams), bananas, and plantains are in this category.

Make those five to nine servings a day count by using the Top 10 "Super Foods" to meet your goal. Enjoy deep green cruciferous vegetables like broccoli, kale, collard greens, bok choy, and spinach. Add color to your plate with carotenoid‐rich foods such as pumpkin, carrots, and toma‐toes. Savor the rich sweetness of deeply colored fruits—strawberries and other berries, watermelon, and oranges. Try to eat most of your servings from whole fruits or vegetables rather than juice.

Starchy and Protein-Rich Plant Foods

Starchy plant foods such as cereals, rice, or pasta, or protein-rich plant foods such as beans, also have a place on your plate. Examples of one serving include the following:

* 1 slice of bread
* 1 ounce ready-to-eat cereal (about 1 cup)
* ½ cup cooked cereal, rice, or pasta
* ½ cup cooked (dried or canned) beans
* 1 medium banana or potato

The goal is to eat four to eight servings of starches each day from unprocessed foods such as starchy vegetables, legumes, or whole grains.

Fats

As we've discussed, monounsaturated fats, essential fatty acids such as omega-3 fats, and polyunsaturated fats are important additions to a healthy diet. Good sources of these fats include monounsaturated oils such as olive or canola oil; cold-water fish such as salmon, sardines, trout, herring, and mackerel; nuts and seeds; avocados; and olives. Other sources of fat include dairy products such as yogurt, milk, and cheese. Choose low-fat varieties of these foods if possible.

Foods that equal 1 teaspoon of fat (5 grams), or one serving:

* 2 ounces lean meat (skinless chicken or turkey, pork, tuna)
* 1 ounce medium-fat meat (beef, 1 egg, skin-on chicken or turkey, fish)
* 1 cup low-fat (2 percent) milk or cottage cheese
* 2 cups skim (1 percent) milk or cottage cheese
* 2 teaspoons salad dressing

Meat: Not the Center of the Plate
*

In a primarily plant-based diet, meat does not play a big role. The New American Plate is two-thirds or more plant-based foods, so meat is a side dish. Experiment with stir-fry recipes, using meat as a flavor booster (try Mushroom Asparagus Stir-Fry with Bay Scallops, page 164). Cancer experts recommend limiting meat intake to one 3-ounce (boneless, cooked weight) portion per day. That amount of meat is about the size of a deck of cards. Eat less red meat and more fish, poultry, and beans. Select lean cuts of meat and broil, poach, or bake them.

* 1 teaspoon peanut butter
* 1 teaspoon oil, butter, margarine, or mayonnaise
* ⅛ avocado
* 12 peanuts
* 5 ounces tofu
* 6 almonds or cashews

To find out how much fat you should consume each day, see "How Much Fat?" on the opposite page.

Maintaining a Healthy Weight

Being overweight or obese can contribute to cancer risk, particularly colon cancer and postmenopausal breast cancer, as well as cancers of the endometrium, pancreas, prostate, and kidney.

Excess body fat may promote and speed the development of cancer in the following ways:

* Causing the body to secrete more of certain hormones, including estrogen, which create an environment that is favorable to cancer development

* Becoming incorporated in cell membranes and changing them so that they lack the defenses they need to block entry of carcinogenic substances

* Decreasing the function of certain components of the immune system

Diabetes, heart disease, and hypertension are also linked to being overweight. When you're overweight, the extra fat cells make the body's tissues less sensitive to the effects of insulin, so your body produces increasing amounts of insulin. Too much insulin can lead to more rapid division of cells, and increased cell replication increases the risk that a random cell will mutate and lead to cancer. Maintaining a healthy weight can reduce the risk of insulin resistance and cancer.

IDENTIFYING YOUR CALORIE GOAL

Here's a formula to help you determine a healthy calorie goal:

* Underweight adults: multiply your body weight (in pounds) by 18.

* Normal-weight adults: multiply your body weight by 16.
* Overweight adults: multiply your body weight by 14.

You now have an estimate of the number of calories you need per day. For example, a 140-pound underweight adult needs about 2,520 calories a day. A 140-pound normal-weight adult needs about 2,240 calories a day. An overweight 140-pound adult needs about 1,960 calories a day. You'll consume more calories on some days and less on others. The idea is to average the target of calories.

HOW MUCH FAT?

Now that you have an idea of your daily calorie requirement, check the following chart to see how many grams of fat you should be consuming. Choose whether you want to eat 20 percent, 25 percent, or 30 percent of your total calories in fat.

> If you are in treatment, don't make weight loss a goal. Focus on getting the best nutrition possible.

Remember, 30 percent is okay if you need to gain weight. Otherwise, 25 percent or 20 percent are great goals for maintaining a healthy weight and maximizing overall health.

As an example, let's say you need 2,000 calories per day and you want to keep your fat intake down to 20 percent of your daily calories. According to the chart, you'll want to consume about 40 grams (about 8 teaspoons) of fat per day, primarily from healthy fats.

Fat Intake

Total daily calories	20% total calories	25% total calories	30% total calories
1,600–1,800	36–40 fg*	44–50 fg	53–60 fg
1,800–2,000	40–44 fg	50–56 fg	60–67 fg
2,000–2,200	44–49 fg	56–61 fg	67–73 fg
2,200–2,400	49–53 fg	61–67 fg	73–80 fg
2,400–2,600	53–58 fg	67–72 fg	80–87 fg

*=fat grams

Here are some hints for maintaining a healthy weight, from a report by the American Cancer Society:

Soft cheeses include Brie, Camembert, feta (goat cheese), blue-veined cheeses like Roquefort, and Mexican soft cheeses like queso blanco.

✻ When you eat away from home, choose foods that are low in fat, calories, and sugar, and avoid large portions.

✻ Eat smaller portions of high-calorie foods. Be aware that "low-fat" or "nonfat" does not mean that the food is low in calories; low-fat cakes, cookies, and similar foods are often high in calories.

✻ Instead of eating calorie-dense foods such as French fries, cheeseburgers, pizza, ice cream, and doughnuts, eat fruits, vegetables, and other low-calorie foods.

Protecting Yourself Against Food-Borne Illnesses

Along with eating a balance of healthy food, creating a healthier diet involves practicing food safety.

Food safety is particularly important for many cancer survivors. If you have a weakened immune system, your body is less effective at protecting you against illnesses carried by bacteria found in foods. Animal products in particular may contain harmful bacteria and other potentially dangerous pathogens. Remember, you cannot rely on your senses to determine if food is contaminated. Spoiled foods do not necessarily change in smell, taste, or appearance. Food can be unsafe to eat before it begins to smell.

The U.S. Department of Agriculture and the American Institute for Cancer Research offer some suggestions to help you and your family lower the risk of getting food-borne illnesses.

SHOPPING

Check the "sell by" and "best used by" dates on the product. The further ahead the date is from the date you are shopping, the better. For fresh meat, poultry, and seafood, buy the item only if the date on the package is today's or yesterday's date.

Buy only refrigerated eggs, and check for clean, uncracked shells. When shopping, buy eggs, milk, meats, fish, and frozen foods last.

STORING

Store eggs in their original carton in the main section of the refrigerator. Refrigerate or freeze meat, poultry, or fish as soon as you get home. Few food-borne bacteria can grow in the refrigerator, and none can grow in the freezer.

Websites: Check the list of helpful and reputable Internet resources in "Getting the Help You Need," page 46.

To prevent contamination, refrigerate leftovers within two hours after cooking or serving. Use these recommended storage times as a guide for keeping foods:

	In Refrigerator	In Freezer
Fresh meat	3 to 5 days	6 to 12 months
Hamburger	1 to 2 days	3 to 4 months
Fresh fish	1 to 2 days	2 to 3 months
Milk	5 days past carton date	1 month
Leftovers	1 to 2 days	2 to 3 months
Eggs	3 to 5 weeks	Do not freeze in shell

PREPARING OR COOKING

Avoid cross-contamination by using separate dishes, cutting boards, and utensils for preparing raw meat, fish, or poultry. Don't chop salad vegetables on a cutting board that you've just used to trim raw meat, poultry, or fish. Wash the cutting board, countertop, utensils, and your hands with hot, soapy water after contact with fresh meats. Change sponges and dish towels often.

Read the expiration dates on food products and look for signs of spoilage. Some food may be unsafe to eat even if it looks and smells fine. When in doubt, throw it out.

Be cautious about foods that may harbor unhealthy bacteria, such as soft cheeses and cold-smoked salmon. Thoroughly reheat cold cuts, and cook hot dogs completely.

Thaw frozen items in the microwave or refrigerator, not on the kitchen counter. Carefully rinse fruits and vegetables. Completely cook foods, using a food thermometer to ensure that meat is thoroughly cooked.

Before using eggs, make sure there are no visible cracks in the shell. Then cook them until the yolk and white are firm. Cook sauces, custards, or casseroles that contain eggs to 160°F. Avoid eating foods that contain raw eggs, such as homemade Caesar dressing, ice cream, mayonnaise, and eggnog.

Avoid eating sprouts (like alfalfa sprouts or sprouts of other seeds). The seeds may be contaminated with *E. coli* or salmonella bacteria.

Cook meats until they reach the correct temperature: 160°F for ground meats like hamburger, 180°F for chicken and turkey—either whole or in pieces. Cook fish until the flesh is opaque and flakes easily. Use a meat thermometer, placed in the thickest part of the food, to test the temperature.

For cooking or heating foods in the microwave, be cautious about using plastic containers. Certain types of plastic, when heated, release compounds that may be harmful to human health. For example, some of these compounds can mimic the action of estrogen in the human body and may contribute to breast cancer and other hormone-sensitive cancers. To avoid this potential problem, use glass containers and microwave-safe lids to reheat your leftovers. Avoid letting any kind of plastic wrap touch the food.

Wrap and refrigerate leftovers within two hours—the sooner the better.

SAFER GRILLING

Animal foods, such as red meat, poultry, and fish, produce cancer-causing compounds when barbecued or cooked on hot stones. Called heterocyclic amines (HCAs), these compounds cause tumors in animals and may increase the risk of cancer in humans.

Don't mothball your barbecue, however—there are steps you can take to minimize the formation of these compounds when you grill:

* Marinate meats before grilling to reduce HCAs. Use about ½ cup of marinade for every pound of food.

* Keep the meat portions small for shorter grilling time.

* Trim the fat from meats. When meat fat drips onto coals, polycyclic aromatic hydrocarbons (PCAs) are formed, which may cause cancer.

* Don't eat any charred or burned portions of meat.

* Grill fruits and vegetables. These foods do not produce HCAs.

Coping with Possible Side Effects of Cancer Treatment

CANCER, ITS TREATMENT, and the worry and fear that accompany the whole experience may result in some side effects that make eating more difficult and food less appealing.

Side effects vary from person to person and can even vary during different phases of treatment and recovery. (Some people don't experience any symptoms, or have just minor ones.) As a result, ways to overcome or minimize side effects also vary. Here are some possible solutions; keep trying different approaches until you find the ones that work best for you.

It may be helpful to keep a journal of your symptoms and side effects. Use a little notebook (or a personal digital assistant, like a Palm Pilot) that you keep with you at all times—in your purse or briefcase during the day, and beside your bed at night. Jot down notes about what seems to trigger side effects, remedies that work and don't work, and questions to ask your doctor, nurse, or nutritionist.

For Nausea, Choose Foods Like These:
Clear liquids, flat soda, or ginger ale
Frozen juice cubes
Fruits or vegetables that are soft or bland (try puréed foods or jarred baby foods)
Oatmeal
Pretzels
Sherbet or sorbet
Skinned chicken (baked or broiled, not fried)
Toast and crackers
Yogurt

Be sure to keep your doctor informed about the side effects you are experiencing. Books, support groups, and the Internet may give you opportunities to discover and share tips and encouragement with other cancer survivors. And remember: Most side effects go away when the treatment comes to an end.

Below are some tips for managing treatment-related symptoms.

NAUSEA

✻ Call your doctor if you feel nauseated. It's better to treat the problem before vomiting begins.

✻ Keep track of when you experience nausea and its possible cause (time of day, foods eaten, events, surroundings). Share this information with your caregivers and medical staff.

✻ Ask your doctor or nurse about medication to help control nausea before and after treatments.

✻ Talk to your nutritionist about ways to modify your diet to minimize symptoms.

✻ Ask family or friends to shop for groceries and cook for you if the sight or smell of food nauseates you. Stay out of the kitchen, or even leave the house, while meals are being prepared.

✻ Try cold foods, which tend to have fewer odors than hot foods.

✻ Experiment with foods and beverages that you have been able to tolerate when you've had the flu, morning sickness, or nausea caused by stress in the past.

✻ Listen to your body. Some people find that they need to avoid fatty, greasy, or fried foods; spicy, hot foods; foods with strong odors; and very sweet foods. Other people crave spicy foods and strong flavors.

✻ Avoid your favorite foods when you're feeling nauseated. You may develop a permanent dislike for them if you link them with feeling sick.

✳ Eat small meals slowly and frequently (every two to three hours).

✳ Rest, sitting up, for about an hour after meals.

✳ Drink or sip cold beverages throughout the day, except at mealtimes. Ginger and peppermint teas may be soothing, and they're good combined.

✳ Keep crackers beside your bed to nibble before getting up in the morning.

✳ Keep your mouth clean. Brush at least twice a day.

✳ If you're hospitalized, have the lids removed from your meals before the tray is brought into your room so most of the odors are dispersed in the hallway.

Recipe for Ginger Tea
✳
1. Wash, peel, and chop a fresh, 1-inch piece of ginger root.
2. Boil the chopped ginger in about 3 cups of water for 20 minutes.
3. Cool and drink the liquid. You may store the tea for a day, but if you have time, it's best made fresh each day.

✳ Ask your doctor or nurse about the use of acupressure bands on your wrists. They may help decrease your nausea.

✳ Wear loose-fitting clothing.

✳ Breathe fresh air, or try relaxation techniques such as meditation or listening to soothing music.

Ginger

Ginger *(Zingiber officinalis)* is an herb recognized to help with nausea associated with chemotherapy. Try drinking ginger tea or flat ginger ale. (If your blood-clotting ability is impaired while undergoing chemotherapy, check with your health care team before using this herb.)

VOMITING

✳ Call your doctor if vomiting continues for longer than half an hour.

✳ Wait an hour after vomiting stops before eating or drinking.

✳ Drink small amounts of clear liquids beginning one hour after vomiting has stopped. A teaspoon every 10 minutes is a good place to start, then gradually increase to a tablespoon every 20 minutes, then 2 tablespoons every 30 minutes. Ginger tea, diluted juices, or clear broth are good choices.

✳ Begin with a liquid diet of teas and broths and gradually work up to a soft diet of applesauce, mashed or sweet potatoes, well-cooked vegetables, oatmeal, skinless chicken, fish, and rice.

CONSTIPATION

✳ Drink 8 to 10 glasses of liquid every day. Try keeping a bottle of water with you at all times. Add lemon, orange, or lime to the water to give it a refreshing flavor. You can also spike the water with fruit juice. Start with equal parts of unsweetened fruit juice and water, and gradually make the mix with more water and less juice.

✳ Drink a warm beverage about half an hour before your usual time for a bowel movement. Try to drink it at about the same time every day to help your body establish a regular routine. Some people find that drinking warm lemon water or prune juice is helpful.

✳ Eat high-fiber foods such as raw fruits and vegetables, whole grains, and nuts. If you have trouble chewing raw fruits and vegetables, try grating or cooking them, skins and all.

✳ Add stewed prunes and raisins to your foods, or eat dried fruit as a snack.

✳ Add oat or wheat bran to foods such as casseroles and homemade breads. Consuming 2 tablespoons of wheat bran a day will make your stools softer and easier to pass. However, because bran absorbs water, make sure you drink at least eight glasses of water a day.

✳ Use ground flaxseed, up to 3 tablespoons a day. Flaxseed is an excellent source of fiber and has a mild laxative effect. Grind the seeds in a coffee mill or blender, and then store the ground meal in a jar in the refrigerator or freezer. Sprinkle the ground meal on cereal, toss it on salads or cooked vegetables, or stir it into soups. Flaxseed has a slightly nutty consistency but a neutral flavor. Start with 2 teaspoons of the ground seed, and gradually add more.

✳ Try to move your bowels at your usual times. Many people find that after breakfast is a good time to try to have a bowel movement.

* Ask your doctor, nurse, or nutritionist if you might need milk of magnesia or a magnesium supplement, a bowel regulator such as Metamucil or psyllium, a laxative or stool softener, or a combination of a laxative and stool softener.

* Take medications as instructed to prevent constipation.

* Get as much light exercise, such as walking, as your condition allows.

* Some pain medications can cause constipation. Talk to your doctor, nurse, or nutritionist before this problem becomes serious.

How to Use Herbs to Help with Diarrhea
*

Brew raspberry leaves as a tea, chew 3 tablespoons of dried blueberries, or make a drink by boiling crushed fresh blueberries in water for 10 minutes. Strain the fruit and drink. Avoid eating fresh blueberries; they may increase your diarrhea.

DIARRHEA

* Call your doctor if you experience more than one episode of diarrhea each day or if diarrhea is persistent.

* Stick to a clear-liquid diet for 12 to 14 hours after an acute bout of diarrhea.

* Increase your intake of liquids to six 8-ounce glasses per day unless your doctor or nurse has instructed you otherwise.

* Drink liquids between meals, not during meals.

* Consume plenty of liquids and foods that contain sodium and potassium. These minerals are often lost when you have diarrhea. Bouillon or fat-free broth, bananas, peach or apricot nectar, and boiled or mashed potatoes are good choices.

* Pass up beverages and foods that contain caffeine, such as coffee, strong tea, caffeinated sodas, alcohol, and chocolate.

* Avoid greasy foods.

* Stay away from foods with a high fiber content, such as fresh fruits, fresh vegetables, and whole-grain cereals and breads.

* Consume foods warm or at room temperature.

* Drink tea and eat applesauce, baby foods, flavored gelatin, and toast. Cheese and cottage cheese are also good choices, but first rule out

Watermelon Popsicles

1 cup seedless watermelon
chunks
1 cup unsweetened orange
juice
1 cup water

❶ Combine all ingredients together in a blender, mixing until smooth. Pour into small paper cups.

❷ Place in the freezer and, when partially frozen, insert popsicle sticks or small plastic spoons for handles.

❸ When completely frozen, unmold by pouring hot water over the bottoms of the cups.

lactose intolerance as the cause of the diarrhea. Foods that are easy to digest and produce fewer residues will give the colon a chance to rest and heal.

✳ Eat small amounts throughout the day, rather than large meals.

✳ Ask your doctor or nurse if you should use Imodium A-D (an over-the-counter medicine for loose stools).

✳ Try herbal approaches to diarrhea. Herbal experts recommend herbs high in tannins, like raspberry leaves and dried blueberries. The tannins in these fruits act as astringents to reduce intestinal inflammation.

SORE MOUTH OR THROAT

✳ Keep your mouth clean. Brush your teeth after eating and at bedtime. Use a soft-bristle, narrow toothbrush and a sodium bicarbonate (baking soda) toothpaste with fluoride added. Dip the toothbrush bristles in very warm water to make them softer. Floss your teeth at least once a day after brushing.

✳ Do not wear loose-fitting dentures.

✳ Do not use mouthwashes that have alcohol in them.

✳ Use cocoa butter, petroleum jelly, lip balm, or a water-based mouth moisturizer to keep your lips moist. Do not use lemon and glycerin swabs.

✳ Try eating fresh or frozen watermelon. The high water content of the melon is very soothing.

✳ Eat a well-balanced diet. Include foods that are high in protein, such as dairy products, poultry, meat, and fish.

✳ Choose soft foods:

Applesauce, bananas, or canned fruits

Cottage cheese

Custards, puddings, and flavored gelatin

Liquids

Mashed potatoes, sweet potatoes, or macaroni and cheese (try Cottage-Style Macaroni and Cheese, page 203.)

Milkshakes, or our Yogurt Protein Shake (page 72) or Fresh Fruit Smoothies (page 70). Tofu can be added to smoothies, or you can make tofu shakes.

Oatmeal or other cereals cooked in nonfat milk or soymilk for added protein (try Great Grains Breakfast Cereal, page 73).

Peach, pear, and apricot nectars

Puréed meats, tofu, or beans

Scrambled eggs

Soft or puréed vegetables

✳ Avoid irritating foods, such as citrus fruit or juice, spicy or salty foods, and hard, crunchy, dry foods (such as raw vegetables and toast), as well as alcohol and tobacco.

✳ Cook foods until they are soft and tender, then cut them into small pieces.

✳ Mix foods with low-fat yogurt, low-fat sour cream, or gravies and sauces made with fat-free broth and thickened with cornstarch. This will make them easier to swallow.

✳ Eat foods cold or at room temperature, rather than hot.

✳ Try tilting your head back or moving it forward while swallowing if you find that swallowing is difficult or painful.

✳ Drink plenty of fluids to avoid becoming dehydrated.

✳ Use a straw for drinking.

Try Honey for a Sore Throat
✳

A cancer support care study found that patients who swallowed honey before and after radiation treatment experienced significantly reduced oral mucositis (sore throat). Participants slowly swallowed 4 teaspoons (20 milliliters) of honey 15 minutes before and after treatment, and then again 6 hours after treatment.

* Drink slippery elm tea or use slippery elm lozenges. The herb slippery elm is a mucilage (soft, moist, and viscous) that coats inflamed tissues.

* Try eating honey if you have a sore throat due to radiation treatment for oral or esophageal cancer.

* Rinse your mouth frequently during the day. Use a saltwater wash: add ½ to ¾ teaspoon of salt to 1 quart of water.

* Ask your doctor about anesthetic lozenges, sprays, or gargles that will numb your mouth and throat long enough for you to eat meals. Also, ask your doctor about using a mixture of equal parts viscous xylocaine, Maalox, and elixir of Benadryl or Gelclair to protect the inside of the mouth. These products require a prescription from your doctor.

* Do not hesitate to ask your doctor about a pain medication for your sore mouth.

LACTOSE INTOLERANCE

Lactose intolerance means that your body can't digest milk sugar—lactose—found in milk products. Symptoms of this condition may include gas, diarrhea, cramping, or nausea after consuming dairy products. To minimize symptoms, try the following:

* Experiment with getting protein and calcium from sources other than milk products. Soymilk, tofu, soy cheese, and soy yogurt are good substitutes for diary. Lactose-free or Lactaid-type milks such as acidophilus milk can often be consumed without causing symptoms.

* Use fermented or cultured reduced-fat milk products such as buttermilk, sour cream, and yogurt. They are often easier to digest than whole milk.

✻ Read labels carefully. Lactose is often used as a filler in products such as instant coffee and some medicines.

✻ Ask your doctor, nurse, or nutritionist about pills for lactose intolerance.

✻ For many people, symptoms of lactose intolerance disappear a few weeks or months after treatment ends or when the intestine heals. Others will need to avoid dairy products indefinitely.

> "It was hard to find something to drink [during treatment]. Even water tasted bad. Then I found that mixing grape juice and soda water to cut the sweetness was okay."

LOSS OF APPETITE

✻ Don't panic. Your appetite will come back when you're feeling better.

✻ Try to eat on a regular schedule and each time you feel hungry. Several small meals throughout the day may work better for you than three big meals. Even a few bites of food or sips of liquid every hour or so can help you get the protein and calories you need.

✻ Plan your largest meals for breakfast or lunch if, like many cancer patients, your appetite is better earlier in the day. Try dinner foods at breakfast time and breakfast foods at dinnertime.

✻ Drink plenty of fluids, even if you can't eat much, so you don't become dehydrated.

✻ Try to limit fluids right before eating; they may decrease your appetite.

✻ Add variety to your menu. Try new recipes and new ways of preparing old favorites, or eat in a restaurant occasionally.

✻ Arrange food attractively and create a pleasant environment. Eat with other people, if possible.

✻ Eat from a small plate with small portions; a large plate with large portions may seem overwhelming. When you're eating out, ask for an extra plate, and then spoon small portions onto it and eat from that. Or ask for a half portion.

✻ Don't hurry your meals. Relax and try to enjoy them.

✻ Talk to your doctor, nurse, or nutritionist about your symptoms.

They may suggest medications to stimulate your appetite, such as Megace or Marinol.

LOSS OF WEIGHT

* Don't waste your appetite eating empty calories.

* Select high-protein, nutrient-rich foods if you're being encouraged to eat a lot of calories. Choose milkshakes made from soymilk and/or tofu instead of ice cream, peanut butter or almond butter instead of butter spread on bread or waffles, and avocado instead of mayonnaise in a sandwich or on toast. Add whey or soy protein powder to smoothies, shakes, and soups.

* Add 2 teaspoons of dry skim milk powder per cup of milk called for in recipes to increase protein and calories without increasing fat content.

* Avoid drinking fluids before meals or filling up on soup or salad at the beginning of meals. Save your appetite for calorie-dense foods.

* Exercise about half an hour before meals to stimulate your appetite, but don't overdo it.

* Dine with friends or family members if possible. Most people eat more when they eat with other people than when they eat alone.

* Eat meals while you watch a favorite TV program or a great video. Distract your mind so you won't think about eating.

WEIGHT GAIN

* Remember that with some cancers, such as breast cancer, it's common for people to gain weight with therapy. Be aware that there may be nothing you can do to control the weight gain. Dieting during treatment is generally not recommended. It's better to focus on healthy eating and physical activity.

* Consume plenty of water—six to eight glasses a day.

* Drink warm fluids such as tea or soup about 20 minutes before meals.

* Try six small meals a day rather than three big ones.

* Eat regularly instead of waiting until you are too hungry.

* Choose more high-fiber foods: fruits, vegetables, beans, and whole grains.

* Keep a journal of what—and when—you eat. Notice when you are eating because you're stressed or bored rather than hungry.

* Fill a small plate rather than a large one, to create the illusion that you're eating more than you are.

* Get as much exercise as your condition allows.

CHANGES IN SENSE OF TASTE

* Experiment to find which foods taste best. Many people think that bland food is what they should be eating, but it's often the strong, spicy foods that sound and taste good. One person even reported craving sauerkraut.

* Marinate meat, fish, and chicken to intensify the flavor.

* Choose moist foods like pasta and stews (try the Seafood Stew with Tomatoes and Saffron on page 167).

* Use more or stronger seasonings such as garlic, onion, and ginger to add flavor.

* Eat tart foods, such as oranges or lemonade, which may have more taste.

* Try new and different foods. While some of your favorite foods may not taste as good for a while, there's a good chance that other foods, even some you haven't liked in the past, will be appealing. Discover new favorites.

* Eat chicken, turkey, eggs, or dairy products—foods that don't have strong odors—rather than beef and pork.

* Use plastic utensils if you're bothered by a metallic taste.

FATIGUE

Fatigue is the most common side effect of cancer treatment. Cancer-related fatigue feels different from other kinds of fatigue; it is often more severe, lasts longer, and isn't relieved by sleep. In a word, it can be overwhelming. Generally, cancer-related fatigue diminishes, but that may take up to a year. Talk with your health care provider about your fatigue; it may be due to a treatable condition such as anemia.

HERE ARE 10 TIPS TO HELP YOU COPE WITH CANCER-RELATED FATIGUE.

✱ Power snack. Eating small meals or a snack every three to four hours will help keep your energy level constant. Try ¼ cup of nuts or seeds, whole-grain crackers topped with 2 teaspoons of peanut butter, or 2 tablespoons of hummus as a dip with baby carrots to boost energy. Eat more when you're feeling well.

✱ Cut the caffeine. Caffeine-containing beverages and products—such as coffee, colas, and chocolate—can mask your fatigue. Instead, drink green or black tea. Tea has only half the caffeine of coffee and is rich in cancer-fighting compounds called polyphenols.

✱ Fluids, fluids, fluids. Dehydration can add to cancer-related fatigue. Your body excretes approximately 3 quarts of water each day through perspiring, breathing, and urinating, and more if you exercise heavily. You can get approximately 1 quart of your water needs through food if you eat a diet rich in fruits and vegetables. The other 2 quarts (8 to 10 cups) should come from fluids, including pure water.

✱ Focus on whole foods. Stock your kitchen with fiber-rich whole foods, including fruits, vegetables, whole grains, and legumes. Whole foods provide optimum energy. Foods high in simple sugars, such as cookies, candies, and processed white flour, rob your body of vital nutrients that fuel energy processes. Use healthy convenience foods for quick meals and snacks: make a no-fuss salad with bagged organic greens, or use frozen vegetables for an easy stir-fry. Prepare and freeze meals ahead whenever possible. Label and date them before freezing.

✱ Keep moving. Physical activity can relieve stress that adds to cancer-related fatigue. Buddy up with a friend to take walks on a regular basis. Or bite-size your activity goal into small segments: take a 10-minute walk at lunch, or use light-resistance weights or bands for spot strength training while you watch television.

✳ Accept help. Give yourself permission to let friends and family members help you. Prepare a list of tasks that friends can do so you can have them ready when they ask (see page 46 for some suggestions). Delegate heavy work. Arrange for Meals on Wheels, a personal chef, or a food delivery service. Use Web-based or telephone grocery delivery services and restaurant delivery in your area.

✳ Get organized. Spread your tasks over the week. Make a list when shopping, organized by store aisle. If you work, organize your clothes the night before.

✳ Keep it simple. Take a shower rather than a bath; it requires less energy. Use warm water rather than hot water because it conserves your body's energy. Use a terrycloth robe after a shower rather than towels. Bring your foot to your knee when putting on shoes so you don't need to lean over. Wear slip-on shoes. Wear button-front shirts rather than pullovers.

✳ Schedule naps. Take short rest breaks in the morning and afternoon, even if you don't feel tired. A 15- or 20-minute nap will boost energy. But balance your naps with adequate sleep and activity. Too much sleep can drain energy.

✳ Breathe and relax. Experiment with breathing exercises, stress-reduction techniques, or meditation if you're having trouble relaxing or sleeping. Try watching funny movies. Call Cancer Lifeline or a similar organization for information about relaxation and stress-management classes in your area. Check with your health care team for treatment options.

Getting the Help You Need

YOU MAY FIND that family and friends are eager to help, especially during the treatment process, but need some direction from you. On the other hand, maybe you don't have family or are physically distant from them, and you need to find out about other available resources. Here are a few suggestions.

Putting Friends and Family to Work

The next time someone asks if there's anything they can do to help, ask them to do one or two of these tasks:

* Plan a week's worth of dinners.
* Accompany you to the grocery store.
* Take your list and go shopping for you.
* Help you prepare vegetables and other foods, or do it for you.
* Prepare a box of healthy, ready-to-eat snack foods.
* Organize friends and/or relatives to cook for you and your family. Each person might be responsible for making meals for one day. It works best if someone other than the cancer patient or caregiver organizes the effort. Meals should be either delivered in disposable containers or labeled so the containers can be returned easily.
* Run errands, such as going to the cleaners, library, post office, or video store for you.
* Pitch in to help with household tasks, such as laundry, vacuuming, yard work, and taking out the garbage.

* Take care of returning phone calls or arranging for bill payment.
* Pick up the kids after school and take them on an enjoyable outing.
* Give the caregiver some time off.
* Take the patient or caregiver for a drive.
* Take the patient to a doctor's appointment.
* Listen.

EXPLORING RESOURCES

* Call an organization like Cancer Lifeline (www.cancerlifeline.org) to find out about services and resources that are available in your community. Services often include transportation, support groups, meal deliveries, legal assistance, and financial aid. Contact your church, the nurse at your doctor's office, the social worker at the cancer center, or a community information line.

* Get connected. Use your computer for fact-finding and information gathering, and for linking up with support groups.

* Find a grocery store and some restaurants in your neighborhood that will deliver to your home. Order groceries online, if that service is available in your area.

* Organize your kitchen so that foods are easy to find and within reach.

* Avoid buying food in hard-to-open containers or in cans if you can't use a can opener.

* Stock up on readily accessible snack foods such as almonds, walnuts, fresh fruit, bean dips, refried beans and tortillas, string cheese, and yogurt.

> **A Note to the Caregiver**
> *
> Keep a variety of foods available and offer them often. However, avoid urging food on cancer patients. They usually know they need to eat and are doing the best they can. What's more, eating may be the one area where they can exert some choice and control over their life.

* Keep ready-to-eat prepared foods on hand for when you're feeling under the weather.

* Turn off the ringer on your phone when you want to rest. Let your voice mail or answering machine take a message.

* Make an effort not to become isolated.

* Reward yourself regularly. Order some flowers along with your groceries, treat yourself to a long-distance telephone call, or get a massage—whatever will give you some pleasure.

* Find new ways to incorporate rest, relaxation, and exercise into your life. Each activity may last only a few minutes, but it will help to invigorate you.

Helpful Websites*

American Cancer Society (ACS) * www.cancer.org
Provides information on ACS programs and events and local ACS chapters.

American Institute for Cancer Research (AICR) * www.aicr.org
American Instute for Cancer Research is a national cancer organization specializing in the field of diet, nutrition, and cancer. On this page you'll find information on cancer and cancer prevention.

Cancer Care * www.cancercare.org
Cancer Care is a national nonprofit organization whose mission is to provide free professional help to people with any type of cancer through counseling, education, information and referral, and direct financial assistance.

Cancer Hope Network * www.cancerhopenetwork.org
The Cancer Hope Network provides support by matching cancer patients with trained volunteers who have themselves undergone a similar experience. Formerly known as CHEMOcare.

The Cancer Survivor's Toolkit * www.cansearch.org/programs/toolbox.html
A free set of audiotapes to help cancer survivors learn how to communicate, find information, solve problems, and advocate. Developed by the National Coalition for Cancer Survivorship, the Association of Oncology Social Workers, and the Oncology Nursing Society.

National Cancer Institute (NCI) ✳ www.cancer.gov

The National Cancer Institute is responsible for conducting and supporting research on cancer. This Web site contains extensive information about the NCI and its programs. A valuable section of the site, called CancerNet, contains a wealth of information about cancer, treatment options, detection, prevention, genetics, supportive care, clinical trials, and a kids' page. There is also a Spanish-language button.

✳ *(From the Cancer Care website.)*

For Caregivers
✳
Be prepared for the tastes of the person undergoing treatment to change from day to day.

Getting Organized

YOU AND YOUR FAMILY may have difficulty finding the time and energy to prepare healthy, nutritious snacks and meals, but eating right is undoubtedly more important now than ever before. The trick is to find ways to make shopping and food preparation as quick and easy as possible.

Stocking up

A good first step is to stock up on supplies that will make wholesome, healthy cooking and eating more convenient. Here are some suggestions for items that might come in handy.

DRY STORAGE

Baking soda and aluminum-free baking powder

Vegetable bouillon and/or broth, low-sodium (powdered or canned)

Canned beans and quick-cooking dried beans, such as split peas and lentils

Canned fruits in unsweetened juice, applesauce, dried fruit

Chicken broth or bouillon, low-fat, low-sodium

Canned tomatoes, low-sodium (purée, paste, sauce)

Cornstarch

Dried mushrooms (shiitakes, morels, chanterelles)

Herbs, spices, and salt-free blends

Jarred spaghetti sauces, hot sauces, and teriyaki sauce

Low-sodium soy sauce, Bragg Liquid Aminos, and Worcestershire sauce

Natural sweeteners like honey, malted grain syrups such as barley malt, molasses, pure maple syrup, Sucanat (unprocessed cane sugar)

Pasta (whole-grain varieties, all shapes and sizes)

Sea vegetables such as nori or kombu

Soymilk, fresh or in shelf-stable cartons

Vinegars (balsamic, rice, red, fruit, white)

Water-packed canned fish—such as salmon, tuna, sardines, or mackerel— and canned chicken

Whole-grain and white flour

Whole grains (brown rice, bulgur, barley, millet, quinoa, polenta, oatmeal, bran)

Whole-grain pancake mixes

REFRIGERATOR STORAGE

Nonfat or low-fat milk and yogurt

Low-fat cottage cheese, ricotta cheese, mozzarella, and cream cheese

Aged cheeses (Parmesan, Asiago, Romano)

Seasoned and plain tofu

Eggs

Spicy mustard

Low-calorie or no-oil salad dressings

Extra virgin olive oil

Fruits and vegetables, organic, seasonal, and locally grown when possible (make the produce aisle a "must" stop when shopping)

Corn and whole-wheat tortillas

Premade, whole-grain breads and muffins

Fresh salsa

Peanut butter and other nut butters (like almond or cashew)

Yogurt, low-fat or nonfat

FREEZER STORAGE

Frozen vegetables

Frozen, unsweetened fruit juice concentrates

Frozen fruits, especially berries

Boneless chicken breasts, lean beef or pork, fish

Nuts, such as almonds, walnuts, Brazil nuts

Seeds, such as pumpkin, sesame, and sunflower seeds

Whole-grain breads, bagels, waffles, premade pizza crusts

Natural juice bars, sorbet, low-fat frozen yogurt

Veggie burgers and soy-based sausages, hot dogs, soy crumbles

Part-skim mozzarella cheese

Handy Utensils and Equipment

IMPORTANT EQUIPMENT

Sharp knives

Mixing bowls

Measuring cups and spoons

Steamer tray or basket

Nonstick skillet and bakeware

Salad spinner

Hand mixer

Blender

NICE, BUT NOT ESSENTIAL

Rice cooker (also excellent for steaming vegetables)

Slow cooker (Crock-Pot)

Food processor

Microwave oven

Popcorn popper

Egg separator

Hand blender

Knife sharpener

Weekly Meal Planning

Make a goal to start creating menu plans. Start with a few of your favorite recipes from this cookbook and plan a week's worth of dinners. As you plan, keep your nutritional goals in mind. For example, "I want to have fish twice a week and meatless meals twice a week. I don't want to cook every night, so we'll go out one night and have leftovers at least once." Create a shopping list that includes all the items you'll need for the meals. By planning ahead, you can shop just once a week. Planning also reduces your chances of resorting to highly processed or fast foods when you're tired and hungry. These foods are often high in fat, salt, and sugar and low in nutrients.

> Every time you make a meal, snap a photo of it before you start eating. Post the photos on the fridge. Soon you'll have your very own food portfolio.

An example of a weekly dinner plan is below. The starred (*) recipes are included in this book.

Save each week's meal plans on your computer or in a notebook or file folder. Favorite plans can be reused when you're short on time or energy. Check websites and vegetarian and ethnic cookbooks for new recipes.

Don't expect to plunge right into writing weekly menus. Instead, you might want to make a commitment to plan one week of dinners this month. Next month, reuse the week of menus you've made, and create one more. Soon you'll have numerous weekly menus from which to choose.

Menus

MENU I

Breakfast: Whole-Grain Pancakes*, fresh cantaloupe slices
Lunch: Pita pocket stuffed with vegetables, drizzled with Cool As a Cucumber Dressing*
Snack: Celery sticks stuffed with nut butter
Dinner: Seafood Stew with Tomatoes and Saffron*, Pecan Honey-Baked Apples*

MENU 2

Breakfast: Yogurt Protein Shake*, Banana Bran Muffin*
Snack: Date Treats*
Lunch: Papaya, Shrimp, and Spinach Salad with Lime Vinaigrette*,
Whole-grain roll, Chocolate Chip Cookies*
Dinner: Creamy Polenta and Bean Casserole*, Honey-Glazed Green
Beans with Almonds*, Baked Custard*

MENU 3

Breakfast: Fresh fruit salad, whole-grain bread topped with nut butter
Lunch: Black Bean Salad*, Chilled Avocado Soup*, rye or sesame seed
crackers
Snack: Low-fat string cheese, fresh grapes
Dinner: Spicy Miso Peanut Noodles*, Garlic-Sautéed Greens*, Berry
Fruit Crisp*

MENU 4

Breakfast: Great Grains Breakfast Cereal* with berries
Lunch: Tasty Tempeh Spread* on a whole-grain bagel, carrot sticks and
red pepper strips, pineapple chunks
Snack: Hummus*, whole-grain crackers
Dinner: Grilled Chicken Skewers with Tangerine-Ginger Glaze*,
organic baby greens with Zesty Tomato Dressing*, Almond-Crusted
Pears in Orange Sauce*

MENU 5

Breakfast: Breakfast Burrito*, tomato juice
Snack: Roasted nuts
Lunch: Basmati Rice with Lentils*, steamed broccoli, sliced kiwi fruit
Dinner: Gingered Carrot Soup*, Ruby Chard with Garlic, Chile, and
Lemon*, crusty whole-grain roll, Raisin-Apple-Date Cookies*

Making Grocery Shopping a Breeze

Planning ahead may seem like more work, but when you know what you're looking for, your grocery shopping gets easier. What's more, you come home with foods you like that will contribute to your good health.

GETTING THE MOST OUT OF YOUR SHOPPING TRIPS

✳ Keep a shopping list handy. Whenever you run out of an item, jot it down. Keep the Top 10 "Super Foods" in mind as you plan your shopping list.

✳ Go to the grocery store once a week with your list. Buy only what's on the list.

✳ Get help from friends or family members.

✳ Shop at nonpeak hours that fit your schedule.

✳ Don't shop when you're hungry. Opt for a healthy snack before going to the store.

✳ During treatment or bouts of fatigue, consider ordering your groceries online, if that service is available in your area. Or find out if your grocery store offers a delivery service.

Organic Food: Is It Better?

According to a study conducted on corn, strawberries, and a type of blackberry called the marionberry, foods that are grown organically have much higher levels of cancer-fighting antioxidants than conventionally grown foods.

To guarantee that consumers get organic foods that are truly grown without synthetic pesticides, fertilizers, antibiotics, or sewage sludge, the U.S. Department of Agriculture has enacted the USDA Organic Rule. When a food displays a USDA "certified organic" seal, this means that it has been grown free of pesticide and sludge, hormones, genetic modification, and germ-killing radiation.

If purchasing organic produce puts a strain on your food budget, learn what foods have the most pesticides and buy them organically grown if possible. The Environmental Working Group publishes a list of the 12 fruits and vegetables with the most and least pesticide residues. Their 2003 survey found that nectarines, pears, and peaches had the most pesticides, while broccoli and peas had low amounts of toxins.

TWELVE FRUITS AND VEGETABLES WITH THE MOST PESTICIDE RESIDUES

Apples

Bell Peppers

Celery

Cherries

Imported Grapes

Nectarines

Peaches

Pears

Potatoes

Red Raspberries

Spinach

Strawberries

TWELVE FRUITS AND VEGETABLES WITH THE LEAST PESTICIDE RESIDUES

Asparagus

Avocados

Bananas

Broccoli

Cauliflower

Corn (sweet)

Kiwi

Mangos

Onions

Papaya

Pineapples

Peas (sweet)

Read Food Labels Before You Buy

The labels on most packaged foods can steer you away from fatty, sugary, or salty products and help you stock your cupboards with more nutritious foods instead. Important things to look for include the following:

✳ Serving size: If you're going to eat the equivalent of two servings, remember to double the figures listed for calories and nutrients.

✳ Calories, and calories that come from fat: Compare these two numbers to figure out the approximate percentage of fat in the product.

✳ Total fat grams: This listing will help you decide if the product is within your "fat budget."

✳ Sodium content: A healthy amount of sodium to consume is between 2,000 and 3,000 milligrams per day.

✳ Total carbohydrates: Check the amount of sugar in the food.

Remember that 4 grams of sugar equals 1 teaspoon. If a product has 32 grams of sugar, it contains about 8 teaspoons of sugar. To check the source of the sugar, look at the food label. The U.S. Department of Agriculture recommends that a 2,000-calorie diet contain no more than 10 teaspoons (40 grams) of sugar per day.

Nutrition Facts		
Serving Size 1 package		
Servings Per Container 1		
		Amount Per Serving
Calories 130	Calories from Fat 0	
		% Daily Value
Total Fat 0g		0%
Saturated Fat 0g		0%
Cholesterol 0mg		0%
Sodium 410 mg		17%
Total Carbohydrate 25g		9%
Dietary Fiber 2 g		7%
Sugars 3g		
Protein 4g		
Vitamin A 30% ● Vitamin C 60%		
Calcium 9% ● Iron 6%		

You'll notice a column entitled "% Daily Value" on food labels. It is designed to tell you how much of a day's worth of fat, carbohydrates, and so forth the product contains. These numbers are based on a 2,000-calorie diet; your own intake may be higher or lower. Use them to give yourself a nutrient-value snapshot of the food.

For example, notice that the dietary fiber daily value (DV) for a 2,000-calorie diet is 25 grams. If a product has 3 grams of fiber, it has 4 percent of the daily requirement. Use this rule of thumb: If a food has 20 percent or more of the DV, consider that food to be high in the DV; low means no more than 5 percent.

It pays to be wary of claims on product packages such as "95 percent fat-free." Hot dogs, luncheon meats, frozen meals, and ice cream, to name just a few, often make these claims, but *beware:* These statements are probably referring to the fat percentage by weight rather than by calories. Fat-free products are not calorie-free, so be careful not to eat too much of them. Don't let the word "fat-free" give you a false sense of security.

You can trust these key words, because they are defined and regulated by the government:

✳ Fat-free: Less than 0.5 gram of fat per serving (remember that fat-free products still contain calories).

* Low-fat: 3 grams of fat or less per serving (except for 2 percent low-fat milk, which has 5 grams per serving).

* Lean: Less than 10 grams of fat, 4 grams of saturated fat, and 95 milligrams of cholesterol per serving.

* Extra lean: Less than 5 grams of fat, 2 grams of saturated fat, and 95 milligrams of cholesterol per serving.

* Very low sodium: 35 milligrams of sodium or less per serving.

* Low sodium: 140 milligrams of sodium or less per serving.

* High fiber: 5 grams of fiber or more per serving.

* Good source of fiber: 2.5 to 4.9 grams of fiber per serving.

IS IT REALLY FAT-FREE?

If you eat two pats of butter, 100 percent of the calories are from fat. Drop two pats of butter in a glass of water, and you've made a beverage that is 96 percent fat-free. But drink it and you'll still swallow the two pats of butter. It doesn't matter to your body whether you eat the butter with or without the water. Either way, you get the same amount of fat.

Avoid products that have added trans fats (they are referred to as hydrogenated or partially hydrogenated oils). There is a direct, proven relationship between trans fats and increased heart disease.

Check the list of ingredients on the package. The most common food additives are sugar and salt, so watch the labels and limit products that include sugar and salt. Other terms indicating sugar include corn syrup, molasses, honey, fructose, sucrose, dextrose, and fruit juice concentrate. Other words for salt include sodium, sodium chloride, sodium bicarbonate, and monosodium glutamate.

For more information about reading food labels, check the Food Labeling and Nutrition website of the Food and Drug Administration: vm.cfsan.fda.gov/label.html.

Simplifying Meal Preparation

Here are some tips for making the cooking and cleanup process as effortless as possible.

✳ Wash and cut up vegetables ahead of time and store in plastic bags in the front of the refrigerator. Use these for quick snacks and meals.

✳ Chop or mince twice as much onion, garlic, or ginger as a recipe calls for and store the rest in a resealable bag in the freezer for later use.

✳ Stop by the salad bar at the grocery store or pick up ready-to-eat vegetables for a stir-fry if your time or energy is limited.

✳ Cook a double batch of rice or beans to use as the core for recipes during the week. Reserve one day a week to cook batches of food.

✳ Double recipes and freeze half in serving-size containers.

✳ Keep prepackaged bags of salad greens or baby spinach handy, along with a supply of healthy convenience foods like canned or dry soups, canned chili, and crusty whole-wheat breads for quick meals. These ready-to-go foods come in very handy when you're not feeling well enough to prepare meals.

✳ If friends or family members ask if there's anything they can do to help, consider suggesting that they prepare some ready-to-eat vegetables or pick up a salad for you at the grocery store.

✳ Use quick and healthy cooking techniques such as these:

Poaching: Simmer foods in hot liquid just below the boiling point. No added fat is needed.

Steaming: Place foods in a steamer basket over boiling water. This helps foods retain their water-soluble vitamins.

Stir-frying: Cook small, uniformly sized pieces of food in a nonstick wok or large skillet, using a small amount of oil, broth, wine, or water.

Microwaving: Use your microwave for defrosting, reheating, and steaming. But be cautious about using plastic containers for cooking or heating foods in the microwave. For more details, see page 32.

Slow cooker (Crock-Pot) cooking: Dig that Crock-Pot out of your storage area. Slow-cooking is an easy way to cook foods like beans, since the cooking can be done overnight and the food is ready the next day.

Grilling: Barbecuing is an easy and fun way to cook, but remember that animal foods such as red meat, poultry, and fish produce cancer-causing compounds when grilled. For some tips for safe grilling, see page 32.

Choosing Fast Foods

When you don't have the time or energy to prepare meals from scratch, or at all, fast foods may be your best available option. Here are some tips for selecting the healthiest restaurant and fast food.

AT RESTAURANTS

Become familiar with menu buzzwords. Ask how the dish is prepared if you are unsure, so that you will know what you're eating. Words that signal unhealthy foods include "fried," "crispy," "creamed," "breaded," "meat sauce," "Alfredo," and "Caesar."

* Ask your waitperson about substitutions. For example, can you have a double order of vegetables instead of French fries with your meal? Can you have your ethnic dish served with fish or steamed tofu instead of beef or pork?

* Avoid fried items, and remove extra fat or skin from meat or poultry. Watch out for added fat from butter, sour cream, or high-fat sauces. Try using flavored vinegar, salsa, low-sodium soy sauce, or fresh lemon juice on foods to enhance the taste.

* At fast-food restaurants, order a grilled chicken sandwich, single hamburger without cheese, salad, veggie burger, or vegetarian burrito.

* Select the salad bar as an alternative to high-fat foods, but go easy on extras that are high in unhealthy fats, such as cheese, mayonnaise-based salads, and bacon bits. Choose an olive oil–based salad dressing and nuts or sunflower seeds and olives as garnishes.

* Order water, iced tea, diet soda, or nonfat milk instead of a shake or whole milk.

* Watch portion sizes. Portion "distortion" is common at restaurants. Order two appetizers as a dinner, or share an entrée with a friend. With super-sized orders, ask your waitperson to bag the leftovers for your next day's lunch.

AT THE GROCERY STORE

Here are some guidelines for choosing from the dizzying array of foods in the freezer aisles.

✳ Select frozen meals that feature vegetables, such as Chinese-style veggies or veggie-and-rice bowls. If the vegetables are listed in the first few items of the ingredient list, you've found a good choice.

✳ Read labels carefully. Choose entrées that contain 15 grams of fat or less and no more than 500 to 800 milligrams of salt per serving. Cut back on products with a high content of sugar and sodium.

✳ Supplement the frozen meal with a bag of frozen vegetables or a bowl of salad greens.

✳ Select foods made with beans, including soy, and whole grains whenever possible.

Ideas for Quick-Fix Meals

BREAKFAST

Hot or cold whole-grain cereal.

Veggie omelet made with egg substitute (try adding garlic, mushrooms, and red or green bell peppers).

Breakfast burrito—scrambled eggs with beans and cheese wrapped in a whole wheat tortilla.

Whole-grain toast topped with nut butter, such as peanut or almond butter, and all-fruit jam.

Frozen whole-grain waffle warmed in the toaster.

Smoothie (juice, yogurt or silken tofu, frozen berries, etc.).

LUNCH

Veggie pita pocket—toss chopped veggies, canned tuna, salmon, or chicken in a whole wheat pita and top with low-fat salad dressing.

Grilled frozen veggie burger (any variety) with tossed salad or a vegetable side dish.

Baked potato topped with chopped vegetables, chili or salsa, and a sprinkle of low-fat cheese.

Whole-grain pasta with tomato sauce and steamed veggies (try broccoli, zucchini, or your favorites).

Hummus with baby spinach stuffed in pita bread.

DINNER

Stir-fried garden vegetables (fresh or frozen) with seasoned tofu or baby shrimp.

Baked yams, sweet potatoes, or squash, topped with peanut sauce or cottage cheese.

Pita pizza—whole-grain pita topped with pizza sauce, lightly steamed veggies, and low-fat cheese, warmed in the broiler or microwave.

Burrito pronto—canned pinto beans, mashed and spread on a whole wheat tortilla. Add shredded lettuce and salsa. Roll up and top with low-fat cheese.

Noodle or rice casserole with chopped leafy greens (such as kale, broccoli, or spinach) and tuna or chicken.

Bean supreme—mix 2 cans of your favorite beans, such as garbanzo and kidney beans, with a can of tomato sauce. Make it spicy (add garlic) or hot (add chile pepper). Heat and add a salad of baby greens.

SNACKS

Celery logs—fill celery sticks with an equal mixture of grated carrots, peanut butter, and crumbled spoon-sized shredded wheat.

Banana sandwich—cut a peeled banana in two, spread one side with nut butter (like peanut butter), and sandwich the two sides back together.

Apricot treats—squeeze the edges of dried apricots to soften them and open them up. Fill each apricot half with a mixture of mashed banana, nut butter, and chopped nuts, rolled oats, or wheat germ.

Apple and peanut butter—cut a medium-sized apple in half. Scoop out the seeds and fill the holes with peanut butter.

Making Favorite Recipes Healthier

RECIPE MAKEOVERS can transform favorite recipes—which may be high in fat, sodium, or sugar—into health-promoting meals. Here are some suggestions for simple, health-boosting recipe changes.

Lowering fat content

✳ Cut the total fat in the recipe in half. For example, reduce ½ cup of olive oil to ¼ cup. Replace the fat with an equal amount of another liquid such as broth, water, wine, buttermilk, or yogurt. Try substituting applesauce, mashed bananas, or puréed prunes for fat if you're making something sweet.

✳ Whenever possible, use vegetable protein such as beans, grains, legumes, and tofu, instead of animal protein. Begin thinking of meat as a condiment rather than the main course.

✳ Start using leaner cuts of meat. Packaging on lean cuts will include the word "loin" or "round"—such as top round or top loin. Substitute skinless turkey or chicken breast in meat recipes. Experiment with soy-based products, like soy crumbles, as a substitute for ground beef. Try using fish in place of fatty meats.

✳ Substitute evaporated skim milk in recipes calling for cream. Use nonfat or low-fat yogurt or sour cream instead of regular sour cream. Try skim or low-fat milk instead of whole milk. Low-fat or fat-free buttermilk is also available and can be purchased in powdered form.

✳ Experiment with nonfat dairy products and low-fat cheese.

✳ Try steaming, broiling, baking, sautéing, or braising. When grilling, remember to marinate animal products to reduce the formation of cancer-causing compounds.

✳ Sauté foods in small amounts of olive oil and extend with broth, water, or wine.

✳ Reduce the amount of full-fat cheeses you use by substituting strong-flavored cheeses like Parmesan or feta.

✳ Substitute two egg whites for every egg called for. Eggs are a source of fat, but all the fat is in the yolk. In baking, try replacing each egg with 2 to 4 tablespoons of soft tofu, puréed with other liquids in the recipe; or combine 2 teaspoons flaxseeds with ¼ cup warm water and whip until foamy in a blender.

Lowering sugar and salt content

The U.S. Department of Agriculture recommends that a 2,000-calorie diet contain no more than 10 teaspoons (40 grams) of sugar. Highly sweetened and processed foods (like some colas, breakfast cereals, baked goods, and candies) can increase insulin response and promote weight gain—and they're full of low-nutrient calories to boot.

Health experts also recommend that you keep your sodium intake under 2,400 milligrams per day (the amount in 6 grams of salt—a little more than a teaspoon). With that in mind, here are a few tips for decreasing sugar and salt in your recipes.

SUGAR

✳ Cut all sugar measurements in half.

✳ Experiment with alternative sweeteners. Familiar ones are applesauce, blackstrap molasses, honey, prune purée, and fruit juice concentrate.

Other sweeteners include rice and barley malt syrup, Sucanat, and date sugar. These can usually be found in the specialty section of large supermarkets or in health food stores. Because date sugar doesn't dissolve in liquid, it's not good in coffee, but it works well for baking.

Making a Sandwich?

✱

Instead of using lettuce, try $1/2$ cup of zesty broccoli sprouts or spinach leaves. Or substitute a veggie or soy-based cheese for dairy cheese.

✱ For every ¾ cup of liquid sweetener substituted for dry sweetener (honey instead of sugar, for example), decrease the amount of liquid in the recipe by ¼ cup, or add an extra ¼ cup of flour.

✱ Frost cakes while still warm with a thin powdered sugar glaze rather than a thick layer of frosting.

SALT

✱ Cut salt measurements in half. If a recipe calls for "salt to taste," add a small amount and then taste. You can always add more if necessary.

✱ Skip or reduce the salt if the recipe calls for baking soda or baking powder. These ingredients already contain sodium.

✱ Get creative with herbs and other seasonings rather than relying on salt. Season vegetables with lemon juice, flavored vinegars, or your favorite low-fat salad dressing.

✱ Remember that all packaged spice mixes (taco, gravy, dressing, stew, spaghetti sauce, etc.) are extremely high in sodium and may contain unhealthy hydrogenated fats. Make your own spice blends, or purchase no-salt blends.

SEASONING SUGGESTIONS

Fruits: Caraway, cinnamon, cloves, ginger, mint, parsley, tarragon

Vegetables: Basil, caraway, chives, dill weed, marjoram, mint, nutmeg, oregano, paprika, rosemary, savory, tarragon, thyme

Salads: Basil, chervil, chives, dill weed, marjoram, mint, oregano, parsley, tarragon, thyme

Rice: Marjoram, parsley, tarragon, thyme, turmeric

Pasta: Basil, fennel, garlic, paprika, parsley, sage
Seafood: Chervil, dill weed, fennel, parsley, tarragon
Poultry: Garlic, oregano, rosemary, sage, savory
Pork: Coriander, cumin, ginger, sage, thyme
Lamb: Garlic, marjoram, mint, oregano, rosemary, sage, savory
Beef: Bay, chives, garlic, marjoram, savory

INCREASING FIBER CONTENT

✱ Choose whole-grain rather than refined flours. You can substitute whole wheat pastry flour for any or all of the white flour a recipe calls for. If you're incorporating other grains such as buckwheat, oats, or amaranth, do not substitute more than a quarter of the total flour called for.

✱ Try pasta products that combine whole wheat flour with white flour—you'll get the benefit of added fiber with a familiar pasta taste.

✱ Use brown rather than white rice, or try a mixture of half white and half brown. Experiment with other whole grains such as quinoa, millet, bulgur, and cornmeal, as suggested in our recipes.

✱ Try whole wheat or corn tortillas for burritos, casseroles, quesadillas, and nachos.

✱ Select a colorful variety of fruits and vegetables, with emphasis on those in our list of Top 10 "Super Foods."

✱ Look for 100 percent whole wheat when buying bread or baked goods. The word "whole" must come before the word "wheat," or you're not getting whole wheat. Don't be fooled by the words "wheat flour," "durum," or "semolina"—these are processed grains. Other grains, such as oats, corn, millet, and quinoa, do not have fiber removed when they are processed, so they don't need to have the word "whole" in front of their names on the label.

SECRETS TO SUCCESS

✻ Change only one ingredient in a recipe at a time. That way, if your creation is less than a success, you'll know where the problem lies.

✻ Start out slowly. You can always further reduce fat, sugar, and salt after your taste buds have adjusted.

✻ Wait to announce the changes until you've served the dish and it has received rave reviews.

✻ Accept progress without perfection. Every journey begins with the first step.

Breakfast

Fresh Fruit Smoothies
Yogurt Protein Shake
Great Grains Breakfast Cereal
Muesli
Whole-Grain Pancakes
Breakfast Burritos
Blueberry Breakfast Cake
Banana Bran Muffins
Applesauce Muffins
Oat and Date Scones
Pumpkin Bread

← Great Grains Breakfast Cereal, page 73

Fresh Fruit Smoothies

From David DeVarona, formerly of Todo Loco Restaurant, Seattle

These combinations of fresh fruit, nonfat yogurt, and ice are blended into cool, smooth, and nutritious drinks. They are great for breakfast, dessert, or snacks. You can turn any of these into an Energy Boost Smoothie by adding 1 teaspoon of protein powder. Once you've mastered the basics, have some fun trying your own variations with your favorite fruits.

Peaches and Cream

½ cup ice

1 peach, peeled, pitted, and quartered

1 banana

2 tablespoons vanilla nonfat frozen yogurt

Orange juice

❶ Place the ice, fruits, and frozen yogurt in a blender. Add orange juice to the 16-ounce line on the blender container.

❷ Blend all ingredients until smooth.

Pineapple Pleasure

½ cup ice

2 spears pineapple, about ¼ of a fresh, peeled pineapple

1 banana

¼ cup vanilla nonfat frozen yogurt

Orange juice

❶ Place the ice, fruits, and frozen yogurt in a blender. Add orange juice to the 16-ounce line on the blender container.

❷ Blend all ingredients until smooth.

Very Strawberry

½ cup ice
½ cup fresh or frozen strawberries
1 banana
¼ cup vanilla nonfat frozen yogurt
Apple juice

❶ Place the ice, fruits, and frozen yogurt in a blender. Add apple juice to the 16-ounce line on the blender container.

❷ Blend all ingredients until smooth.

Serves 1. Per serving: 217 calories, 1 g fat, 4 g protein, 53 g carbohydrates, 4 g fiber, 23 mg sodium

Nutrition Tip
✱
Protein powders come from different sources, including whey, soy, and rice. Whey is derived from dairy sources, so avoid it if you have problems digesting those foods. Soy provides good-quality protein, equivalent to animal protein.

Yogurt Protein Shake

A refreshing, high-protein shake loaded with vitamins, minerals, and fiber, great for breakfast or anytime. Frozen fruit makes the drink thick, almost like an ice cream shake. Try this with any of your favorite berries.

½ cup nonfat yogurt

1½ teaspoons protein powder (made with whey, soy, or egg)

½ cup fresh or frozen fruit, such as cherries, berries, or cut-up peaches or melon

1 banana, fresh or frozen

¼ cup or more fruit juice

1 or 2 pitted dates (optional)

❶ Combine all ingredients in a blender, mixing until smooth. Add more fruit juice, if necessary, to reach the desired consistency.

Serves 1. Per serving: 294 calories, 2 g fat, 10 g protein, 65 g carbohydrates, 5 g fiber, 110 mg sodium

VARIATION

Strawberry Shake

½ cup nonfat strawberry yogurt

½ cup frozen strawberries

½ cup apple juice

1 banana, sliced

1½ teaspoons protein powder

2 pitted dates (optional)

Cooking Tip
*

For variety, substitute vanilla-flavored soymilk for the yogurt or fruit juice. Add 2 ounces soft, silken-style tofu for extra protein, carbohydrates, and fiber. Toss in about a dozen almonds for extra protein and calories.

Great Grains Breakfast Cereal

Cooked whole grains are a good way to start your day. Add 2 to 3 tablespoons of chopped nuts to the cooked cereal, or swirl in a tablespoon of nut butter for added protein. For a breakfast express meal, make this cereal the night before and warm it up in the morning.

4 cups water
1 cup whole oats, buckwheat groats, or cornmeal
1 teaspoon vanilla extract
Seasonal fruit (berries, chopped apples, pears, or other fruit)
Soymilk or nut milk
¼ cup nuts, such as almonds or walnuts, finely chopped

❶ In a medium saucepan, bring the water to a boil; add the grains and vanilla.

❷ Cook over medium heat until the grains are tender but still well defined, 10 to 15 minutes.

❸ Remove from the heat, add chopped fruit, and flavor with soy⁄ or nut milk. Spoon into bowls.

❹ Top each bowl with 1 tablespoon chopped nuts.

Serves 4. Per serving: 155 calories, 3 g fat, 7 g protein, 26 g carbohydrates, 4 g fiber, 582 mg sodium

Tip from Jeanne, a cancer survivor: "I stir applesauce into hot cereal for an added flavor boost."

Muesli

Muesli is a great comfort food that is easily digested and provides sustained energy. Fresh peaches, nectarines, or berries may be served alongside.

1½ cups old-fashioned rolled oats
1½ cups nonfat milk
1½ tablespoons lemon juice
2 Granny Smith or Fuji apples, grated
¼ cup nuts, such as almonds or walnuts, finely chopped
1 tablespoon raisins
½ teaspoon ground cinnamon

❶ Combine the oats and milk in a large bowl. Let stand for 15 minutes.

❷ In a small bowl, sprinkle the lemon juice over the grated apple, then drain.

❸ Stir the apple into the oat mixture.

❹ Spoon into individual serving bowls and sprinkle with nuts, raisins, and cinnamon.

Serves 4. Per serving: 239 calories, 7 g fat, 10 g protein, 38 g carbohydrates, 5 g fiber, 50 mg sodium

Tip from Maribeth, a Cancer Lifeline intern: "I add ½ teaspoon of vanilla to the milk and drizzle ½ teaspoon of honey on top. To save time if I'm rushed in the morning, I use dried chopped apples."

Whole-Grain Pancakes

These fiber-rich, versatile pancakes are a wonderful addition to your breakfast options.

2 cups whole wheat pastry flour
1 tablespoon baking powder
½ teaspoon salt
1 tablespoon sweetener (brown or date sugar or fruit juice concentrate)
3 eggs, separated, or 2 egg whites and 2 whole eggs, separated
2 cups nonfat buttermilk or soymilk (for waffles, reduce the milk to 1¼ cups)
1 tablespoon butter or non-trans fat margarine, melted

Cooking Tip
✳
For variety, try using other whole grains such as oat bran, oat flour, amaranth flour, cornmeal, rolled oats, or buckwheat flour. Consider adding chopped fruit, nuts, or sunflower seeds to the batter.

❶ Preheat a lightly greased frying pan.

❷ Sift together the flour, baking powder, and salt in a medium mixing bowl. Set aside.

❸ In a large bowl, beat together the sweetener, egg yolks, buttermilk, and butter. Mix in the dry ingredients until just moist.

❹ Beat the egg whites to stiff peaks and gently fold them into the batter.

❺ Using a ¼-cup measure, drop the batter onto the hot frying pan, spacing the pancakes well apart. Cook until golden brown on each side.

Serves 6. Per serving: 225 calories, 5 g fat, 11 g protein, 36 g carbohydrates, 5 g fiber, 548 mg sodium

Breakfast Burritos

Breakfast burritos—scrambled eggs and beans wrapped in a tortilla and topped with salsa, sour cream, or plain yogurt—are a popular breakfast item at fast-food restaurants. Simple to make and delicious, this recipe provides a healthy alternative.

2 teaspoons olive oil
½ cup chopped onion
½ green or red bell pepper, chopped
2 cloves garlic, minced
½ teaspoon ground cumin
1 can (15 ounces) nonfat refried beans
4 eggs, beaten (or use 3 egg whites and 1 whole egg)
4 whole wheat tortillas
½ cup nonfat plain yogurt or low-fat sour cream
Salsa

❶ Preheat the oven to 350°F.

❷ In a large skillet, heat the olive oil over medium heat.

❸ Add the onion, bell pepper, and garlic. Sauté until tender. Add the cumin and remove from the heat.

❹ Warm the beans in a small saucepan.

❺ In a medium bowl, whisk the eggs, then pour over the sautéed vegetables. Return to medium heat and carefully stir until the eggs are soft and well scrambled.

❻ Wrap tortillas in aluminum foil and warm them in the oven for about 10 minutes.

❼ Fill each tortilla with a quarter of the eggs and beans. Top with yogurt or sour cream. Add salsa to taste. Roll up the tortilla, folding in the ends to form a burrito. Serve immediately.

Serves 4. Per serving: 361 calories, 10 g fat, 20 g protein, 54 g carbohydrates, 12 g fiber, 623 mg sodium

Blueberry Breakfast Cake

This breakfast favorite features blueberries, one of our Top 10 "Super Foods," in a rich, high-fiber blend of whole-grain wheat and oat flours.

1 large egg

½ cup skim milk

½ cup plain nonfat yogurt

3 tablespoons butter or non-trans fat margarine, melted

½ cup oat flour

1 cup whole wheat pastry flour

½ cup unbleached all-purpose flour

½ cup sugar

4 teaspoons baking powder

½ teaspoon salt

1½ cups fresh or frozen unsweetened blueberries

Topping

3 tablespoons sugar

2 tablespoons finely chopped walnuts

¼ teaspoon ground cinnamon

❶ Preheat the oven to 400°F.

❷ Coat an 8-inch square baking pan with nonstick cooking spray.

❸ In a large mixing bowl, whisk together the egg, milk, yogurt, and butter or non-trans fat margarine.

❹ Mix the oat flour, whole wheat flour, all-purpose flour, sugar, baking powder, and salt in a bowl.

❺ Sift the dry ingredients into the liquid mixture. Stir the batter just to blend. Do not overbeat.

→ *recipe continues*

❻ Fold in the blueberries and turn the batter into the prepared pan.

❼ For the topping, in a small bowl, stir together the sugar, walnuts, and cinnamon. Sprinkle over the batter.

❽ Bake for 20 to 25 minutes, or until the top is golden brown and a knife inserted into the center of the cake comes out clean.

❾ Cool on a rack for 10 minutes. Cut into squares and serve warm.

Serves 9. Per serving: 214 calories, 4 g fat, 6 g protein, 40 g carbohydrates, 3 g fiber, 374 mg sodium

---

Nutrition Tip
*
Blueberries, both wild and cultivated, may be one of the richest sources of plant-derived antioxidants.

Banana Bran Muffins

From Merrilee Buckley, Cancer Lifeline intern

Most muffins are high in sugars and fat—not these fruit- and fiber-rich treats.

½ cup whole wheat pastry flour
½ cup unbleached all-purpose flour
¼ cup sugar
2½ teaspoons baking powder
½ teaspoon salt
1 cup wheat bran
1 egg, well beaten
1 ripe banana, mashed
¼ cup milk
2 tablespoons canola oil
1½ teaspoons ground cinnamon
1 teaspoon vanilla extract

❶ Preheat the oven to 400°F. Spray 10 muffin cups with nonstick cooking spray or line with paper baking cups.

❷ In a large mixing bowl, sift together the whole wheat and all-purpose flours, sugar, baking powder, and salt. Stir in the bran.

❸ Add the egg, banana, milk, canola oil, cinnamon, and vanilla and stir to moisten.

❹ Pour into the prepared muffin tin, filling each cup half full with batter.

❺ Bake for 20 to 25 minutes, or until the muffins spring back when touched in the center. Remove from the tin and allow to cool.

Makes 10 muffins. Per muffin: 125 calories, 4 g fat, 4 g protein, 21 g carbohydrates, 4 g fiber, 264 mg sodium

Applesauce Muffins

From Jean Warren, author of *Super Snacks*

These muffins use only natural sweeteners and make a wonderful breakfast or an easy lunch. Serve with yogurt and fresh fruit.

½ cup raisins
½ cup unsweetened apple juice concentrate
1 ripe banana, sliced
¼ cup canola oil
1 teaspoon vanilla extract
½ cup unsweetened applesauce
1 egg
1 cup whole wheat flour
½ cup wheat germ
½ teaspoon baking powder
½ teaspoon baking soda
¼ teaspoon salt
1 tablespoon ground cinnamon

❶ Preheat the oven to 400°F. Spray a 12-cup muffin tin with nonstick cooking spray or line with paper baking cups.

❷ Heat the raisins and apple juice concentrate in a small saucepan until the raisins are soft (about 3 minutes). Pour into a blender and purée.

❸ Add the banana, canola oil, vanilla, applesauce, and egg to the blender and blend with the raisin purée.

❹ In a large bowl, combine the flour, wheat germ, baking powder, baking soda, salt, and cinnamon and stir well.

❺ Add the wet ingredients to the dry ingredients and stir just until mixed.

❻ Pour into the prepared muffin tin, filling each cup half full with batter.

❼ Bake for 20 minutes, or until the muffins spring back when touched in the center. Remove from the tin and allow to cool.

Makes 12 large muffins. Per muffin: 193 calories, 6 g fat, 3 g protein, 22 g carbohydrates, 3 g fiber, 133 mg sodium

Oat and Date Scones

Scones are traditionally richer than regular biscuits due to the butter and egg. This recipe balances out that richness by being packed with whole grains and fiber, including oat flour.

> 1 cup unbleached all-purpose flour
> ½ cup whole wheat pastry flour
> ½ cup oat flour (place oatmeal in a blender and grind for a
>   minute or so)
> 4 tablespoons brown sugar
> 2 teaspoons baking powder
> ½ teaspoon baking soda
> ½ cup butter or non-trans fat margarine, cut into pieces
> ½ cup chopped dates
> 1 egg, lightly whisked
> ½ cup buttermilk

❶ Preheat the oven to 375°F.

❷ In a large mixing bowl, combine the all-purpose flour, whole wheat flour, oat flour, brown sugar, baking powder, and baking soda.

❸ Using a fork, blend in the butter or non-trans fat margarine until the mixture is crumbly. Stir in the dates.

❹ Add the egg and buttermilk, stirring with a fork until the dough holds together.

❺ Gently knead the dough a few times on a lightly floured board. Do not overmix. Add up to 2 tablespoons more flour if the dough seems too sticky to work with.

6 Shape the dough into a flat 8-inch round. Cut into 8 wedges and arrange 2 inches apart on a nonstick baking sheet.

7 Bake for 20 minutes, or until golden brown. Serve warm.

Makes 8 scones. Per scone: 234 calories, 8 g fat, 5 g protein, 37 g carbohydrates, 3 g fiber, 262 mg sodium

---

Cooking Tip
*
A teaspoon of finely grated orange peel or $1/2$ cup of dried apricots may be substituted for the dates.

Pumpkin Bread

From Margo Elbert, Cancer Lifeline intern

A rich and moist bread that helps you get your daily dose of antioxidant-powered orange vegetables.

1½ cups whole wheat flour
1 cup soy flour
2 teaspoons baking powder
1 teaspoon baking soda
½ teaspoon salt
½ teaspoon ground cinnamon
½ teaspoon ground cloves
½ teaspoon ground nutmeg
¼ cup canola oil
½ cup Sucanat, or evaporated cane sugar
¼ cup honey
2 tablespoons blackstrap molasses
1 teaspoon vanilla extract
1 can (16 ounces) pumpkin
½ cup raisins
½ cup or more chopped walnuts
2 tablespoons millet

❶ Preheat the oven to 350°F. Lightly oil 1 regular loaf pan (9 by 4 inches) or 2 smaller pans.

❷ In a large bowl, combine the whole wheat and soy flours, baking powder, baking soda, salt, cinnamon, cloves, and nutmeg.

❸ In a mixing bowl, beat together the oil, Sucanat, honey, molasses, and vanilla.

❹ Whip in the pumpkin.

5 Blend in the dry ingredients, ½ cup at a time.

6 Fold in the raisins, walnuts, and millet.

7 Spoon into the prepared pan and bake for 50 minutes or slightly longer, until a knife inserted into the center comes out clean.

8 Cool on a rack for 10 minutes before removing from the pan.

Makes 1 loaf, 8 servings. Per serving: 362 calories, 15 g fat, 10 g protein, 53 g carbohydrates, 7 g fiber, 413 mg sodium

---

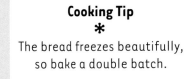

Cooking Tip
✳
The bread freezes beautifully,
so bake a double batch.

Salads and Appetizers

Ray's Cafe Seafood Margarita
Summer Rolls with Red Chili–Peanut Dipping
   Sauce
Hummus
Tropical Salsa
Papaya, Shrimp, and Spinach Salad with Lime
   Vinaigrette
Spinach Salad with Poppy Seed Balsamic
   Vinaigrette
Black Bean Salad
Waldorf Salad
Caesar Dressing
Zesty Tomato Dressing
Cool as a Cucumber Dressing
Olive Oil and Herb Spread
Tasty Tempeh Spread

← Papaya, Shrimp, and Spinach Salad with Lime Vinaigrette, page 96

Ray's Cafe Seafood Margarita

From Chef Charles Ramseyer, Ray's Boathouse Cafe, Seattle

An elegant appetizer that will set the tone for any meal.

4 jumbo prawns, cooked and peeled (size 8 to 12 per pound)
4 ounces cooked bay shrimp
2 ounces cooked Dungeness crabmeat
6 segments of lime
6 segments of orange
½ cup cubed mango
2 tablespoons chopped cilantro
2 teaspoons fresh lime juice
Kosher salt

Garnish

2 radicchio leaves
2 curly endive leaves
Crispy corn chips
Cilantro sprigs

❶ Dice 2 of the jumbo prawns. Butterfly the remaining 2 prawns by cutting them lengthwise down the backs.

❷ In a medium bowl, mix the diced prawns, butterflied prawns, bay shrimp, crabmeat, lime segments, orange segments, mango, cilantro, and lime juice.

❸ Season with salt to taste and marinate in the refrigerator for 15 minutes.

❹ Line 2 chilled margarita glasses with radicchio and endive leaves.

❺ Spoon the mixture into the glasses and garnish with corn chips and cilantro sprigs. Serve immediately.

Serves 2. Per serving: 284 calories, 2 g fat, 42 g protein, 25 g carbohydrates, 4 g fiber, 247 mg sodium

It is within your control to choose how you will respond to the ways cancer will change your life.

Summer Rolls with Red Chili–Peanut Dipping Sauce

From Chef Alvin Binyua, Axis Restaurant, Seattle

These delightful, vegetable-filled rolls can be served warm or at room temperature, steamed or not, accompanied by a lively homemade red chili dipping sauce.

1 tablespoon peanut oil
2 teaspoons minced garlic
2 teaspoons minced fresh ginger
1 cup julienned carrots (matchstick size)
1 cup julienned zucchini (matchstick size)
1 cup julienned snow peas (matchstick size)
1 cup bean sprouts
¼ cup basil leaves, thinly sliced
¾ cup peanuts, chopped (optional)
24 sheets rice paper *(bohn trang)*
Pickled ginger, for garnish
Red Chili–Peanut Dipping Sauce (recipe follows)

❶ Pour the oil into a hot frying pan, add the garlic and ginger, and sauté briefly. Add the carrots, zucchini, snow peas, bean sprouts, and basil, stir-frying for about 30 seconds (the vegetables should still be crunchy). Remove from the heat, add the peanuts, if desired, and set aside.

❷ Soften each sheet of rice paper by dipping it in lukewarm water. Put about 2 tablespoons of the vegetable mixture in the middle of each sheet. Fold the sides over and roll each sheet up tightly. Serve as is with pickled ginger and red chili sauce for dipping, or steam the rolls as described in the next step.

❸ To steam the rolls, place them in a bamboo steamer lined with parchment paper. Steam for 1 minute. Lift out carefully, as the rolls break easily. Lay on a flat surface and cover with a towel. Let sit for 1 to 2 minutes before serving with pickled ginger and red chili sauce.

Serves 12. Per serving: 128 calories, 3 g fat, 5 g protein, 21 g carbohydrates, 1 g fiber, 186 mg sodium

---

Red Chili–Peanut Dipping Sauce

1 cup water
1 tablespoon fish sauce
1 tablespoon red chili paste with garlic
¼ cup firmly packed brown sugar
1 tablespoon cornstarch dissolved in ¼ cup cold water
Juice of ½ lime
2 tablespoons peanuts, chopped
1 tablespoon grated carrot
2 teaspoons chopped fresh basil

❶ Bring the water, fish sauce, chili paste, and brown sugar to a boil in a medium saucepan.

❷ Add the cornstarch/water mixture and simmer gently for 3 to 4 minutes. Remove from the heat and let cool.

❸ Stir the lime juice, peanuts, carrot, and basil into the cooled mixture. Serve as a dipping sauce.

Serves 12. Per serving: 15 calories, 0 g fat, 0 g protein, 3 g carbohydrates, 0 g fiber, 79 mg sodium

---

Hummus

A truly versatile food, hummus can be used as a dip for vegetables, as a sandwich filling, or as a spread on whole-grain crackers.

2 cloves of garlic, or more to taste
2 tablespoons olive oil
1 tablespoon tahini
2 tablespoons fresh lemon juice
1 can (15 ounces) organic garbanzo beans
½ teaspoon salt or sea salt
2 tablespoons or more water

❶ Crush the garlic and place it in a blender or food processor with the oil, tahini, and lemon juice. Blend until smooth.

❷ Add the garbanzo beans and blend.

❸ Add 2 tablespoons water.

❹ Blend for 5 minutes. For a thinner consistency, add more water.

Serves 16. Per serving: 52 calories, 3 g fat, 2 g protein, 5 g carbohydrates, 1 g fiber, 72 mg sodium

Tip from Jenn, who perfected this recipe: "Adding water gives the hummus just the right texture. I start with 2 tablespoons, then add more until I get the smoothness I want."

Tropical Salsa

From David DeVarona, formerly of Todo Loco Restaurant, Seattle

Pair this unique salsa with baked tortilla chips for a fun way to eat fruits.

1 mango, peeled, pitted, and diced
1 pint fresh strawberries, sliced
½ fresh pineapple, peeled and diced
Juice of 1 lime
2 tablespoons chopped cilantro
1 serrano chile pepper, minced (optional)

Place all ingredients in a medium bowl and mix well. Plan to use this salsa within a day; it does not keep well.

Serves 8. Per serving: 44 calories, 0 g fat, 1 g protein, 11 g carbohydrates, 2 g fiber, 1 mg sodium

Cultivate an attitude of kindness and compassion toward yourself.

Papaya, Shrimp, and Spinach Salad with Lime Vinaigrette

From Chef Kathy Casey

An easy-to-prepare salad, this dish has a medley of colors and flavors.

1 head butter lettuce
1 bunch fresh spinach
1 large, firm ripe papaya, peeled, seeded, and diced
1 large orange, peeled and diced
1 large, ripe avocado, diced
½ cup sliced almonds, lightly toasted
8 ounces cooked bay shrimp (optional)
Lime Vinaigrette (recipe follows)

❶ Wash and dry the lettuce and spinach, and cut or tear into bite-size pieces. Place in a large bowl and add the diced papaya, orange, avocado, almonds, and the shrimp, if desired.

❷ Drizzle in ½ cup of the Lime Vinaigrette and toss gently to coat the salad evenly.

❸ Serve immediately, passing the remaining vinaigrette at the table.

Serves 6. Per serving: 314 calories, 21 g fat, 14 g protein, 21 g carbohydrates, 7 g fiber, 384 mg sodium

Lime Vinaigrette

¼ cup Rose's lime marmalade
¼ cup fresh lime juice
2 teaspoons orange juice concentrate
½ teaspoon Dijon mustard
½ teaspoon salt
½ teaspoon ground coriander

⅛ teaspoon cayenne pepper

⅓ cup canola oil

❶ Place the lime marmalade in a medium bowl and stir until the lumps are dissolved.

❷ Add the lime juice and whisk until smooth. Stir in the orange juice concentrate, mustard, salt, coriander, and cayenne.

❸ Slowly whisk in the canola oil. The dressing should be smooth and emulsified.

Makes ¾ cup. Per serving: 140 calories, 13 g fat, 0 g protein, 8 g carbohydrates, 0 g fiber, 209 mg sodium

Chef's Note
*
This salad is also great as an entrée, topped with grilled prawns instead of bay shrimp.

Spinach Salad with Poppy Seed Balsamic Vinaigrette

A special dressing makes this spinach salad stand out from the crowd. In spring and summer, add fresh strawberries. In autumn and winter, try dried apricots.

> Poppy Seed Balsamic Vinaigrette (recipe follows)
> 2 bunches spinach, about 4 cups cleaned
> ½ cup walnuts or hazelnuts, chopped
> 2 tablespoons chopped green onion, for garnish (optional)

Poppy Seed Balsamic Vinaigrette

> 1 tablespoon poppy seeds
> 1 tablespoon sesame seeds
> 2 tablespoons sugar
> ¼ cup balsamic vinegar
> 2 tablespoons olive oil
> 3 tablespoons grape or apple juice (grape adds a nice flavor)
> ½ teaspoon Worcestershire sauce
> ½ teaspoon paprika

❶ For the poppy seed dressing, in a small bowl mix together the poppy and sesame seeds, sugar, balsamic vinegar, olive oil, juice, Worcestershire sauce, and paprika.

❷ To assemble the salad, wash the spinach and tear it into bite-size pieces. Put into a large salad bowl.

❸ Pour the poppy seed vinaigrette over the spinach.

❹ Toss the salad and top with the nuts and the green onions, if desired.

Serves 4. Per serving: 143 calories, 9 g fat, 3 g protein, 15 g carbohydrates, 2 g fiber, 55 mg sodium

Black Bean Salad

From Merrilee Buckley, Cancer Lifeline intern

Bring color to your table with this bright mix of beans, vegetables, and spices.
Serve it with Polenta Squares, page 158.

2 cups canned black beans (one 15-ounce can)
1 cup frozen yellow corn
½ red onion, diced (½ cup)
½ green bell pepper, diced (about ½ cup)
½ red bell pepper, diced (about ½ cup)
2 cloves garlic, minced
2 tablespoons chopped cilantro
2 tablespoons olive oil
2 tablespoons fresh lime juice
1 teaspoon salt
1½ teaspoons freshly ground black pepper
½ teaspoon chili powder
1 teaspoon ground cumin

❶ Mix the beans, corn, onion, green and red bell pepper, garlic, and
cilantro in a medium-sized bowl.

❷ In a smaller bowl, mix the olive oil, lime juice, salt, pepper, chili
powder, and cumin to make a dressing.

❸ Add the dressing to the black bean mixture. Mix well. Refrigerate for
at least 1 hour before serving.

Serves 6. Per serving (¹/₂ cup): 158
calories, 5 g fat, 6 g protein, 23 g
carbohydrates, 7 g fiber, 389 mg sodium

Nutrition Tip
✱
Legumes, like black beans, are
richer in high-quality protein
than most other plant foods.

Waldorf Salad

Enjoy the delightful mixture of textures in this healthy update of the classic salad.

Waldorf Dressing (recipe follows)
2 Red or Golden Delicious apples, chopped
2 Fuji or Granny Smith apples, chopped
2 stalks celery, chopped
1 cup red or green seedless grapes
½ cup walnuts, chopped
½ cup raisins
4 to 6 cups salad greens

Waldorf Dressing

¾ cup plain nonfat yogurt
¼ cup low-fat sour cream
¼ cup low-fat mayonnaise
¼ cup fresh orange juice
¼ teaspoon ground nutmeg

> **Nutrition Tip**
> *****
> Walnuts are a plant source of immune-boosting omega-3 fatty acids and, like all nuts, are also rich in protein.

❶ For the dressing, in a small bowl combine the yogurt, sour cream, mayonnaise, orange juice, and nutmeg.

❷ To make the salad, in a medium bowl combine the apples, celery, grapes, walnuts, and raisins.

❸ Toss the dressing with the apple mixture. Chill.

❹ Serve on a bed of greens.

Serves 6 to 8. Per serving: 205 calories, 8 g fat, 5 g protein, 32 g carbohydrates, 3 g fiber, 80 mg sodium

Caesar Dressing

From Merrilee Buckley, Cancer Lifeline intern

This pure, hearty dressing is a delicious update of a classic recipe. Serve with romaine lettuce, croutons, and grated Parmesan cheese for the traditional favorite taste. Plum tomato slices are a colorful addition.

2 cloves garlic, minced

¼ cup olive oil

1 teaspoon salt

½ teaspoon dry mustard

1 or 2 anchovy fillets, minced, or ½ teaspoon anchovy paste

1½ teaspoons cracked black pepper

3 or 4 drops Worcestershire sauce

2 tablespoons white vinegar

1 tablespoon fresh lemon juice

❶ Place all ingredients in a blender or food processor. Whip until blended.

Serves 4 to 6 (about 2 tablespoons per serving). Per serving: 141 calories, 14 g fat, 0 g protein, 3 g carbohydrates, 0 g fiber, 770 mg sodium

Salad Dressing Hints
*

For nutritious salads, use low-fat dressings. Top carefully selected greens with the freshest ingredients. A squeeze of lemon juice, a splash of wine or balsamic vinegar, or a drizzle of fruit juice can add just the right finishing touch to any salad. Top with a selection of grated Parmesan cheese, garbanzo beans, raisins, or aromatic herbs such as basil, marjoram, oregano, thyme, rosemary, chives, or green onions.

Zesty Tomato Dressing

A delicious alternative to traditional vinaigrettes, this dressing adds a splash of color to salads.

½ cup tomato juice
1 tablespoon olive oil
1 tablespoon fresh lemon juice
1 tablespoon vinegar
¼ teaspoon dry mustard, or 1 teaspoon Dijon mustard
1 tablespoon finely chopped onion
1 teaspoon finely chopped parsley

Combine all ingredients, and mix until well blended.

Serves 8. Per serving: 20 calories, 2 g fat, 0 g protein, 1 g carbohydrates, 0 g fiber, 54 mg sodium

Hope is a crucial part of healing. Never let anyone take your hope away.

Cool as a Cucumber Dressing

A simple, high-protein recipe for salad dressing or vegetable dip. Stuff pita bread with fresh vegetables and drizzle this creamy dressing over the top.

> 1½ cups plain nonfat yogurt with live cultures (see the Nutrition Note)
> ½ cup low-fat sour cream
> 2 cloves garlic, crushed
> 2 tablespoons fresh lemon juice
> 2 tablespoons chopped fresh dill
> ½ medium-sized cucumber, very finely grated
> ¼ cup walnuts, chopped

Blend together all ingredients in a medium-sized mixing bowl. Keep refrigerated until ready to serve.

Makes about 2½ cups. Per tablespoon: 15 calories, 1 g fat, 1 g protein, 1 g carbohydrates, 0 g fiber, 8 mg sodium

Nutrition Note
*

Yogurt can often be consumed by people who are lactose intolerant. Because yogurt with active cultures is predigested, the amount of milk sugars is very low.

Olive Oil and Herb Spread

This mixture is a healthy alternative to butter or margarine. Keep it in your freezer as a handy and tasty spread for bread.

½ cup olive oil

1 tablespoon dried or 2 tablespoons fresh basil, oregano, rosemary, red pepper flakes, or minced garlic

❶ In a small bowl, mix the olive oil with the other ingredients of your choice.

❷ Pour into a cruet and place in the freezer. Store in the freezer between uses.

Makes about ½ cup. Per tablespoon: 120 calories, 14 g fat, 0 g protein, 0 g carbohydrates, 0 g fiber, 0 mg sodium

You do not have to take this journey alone. Pain shared is pain lessened. Consider joining a support group.

Tasty Tempeh Spread

From Margo Elbert, Cancer Lifeline intern

This spread is made with tempeh, a fermented soy product with a smoky, meat-like texture. Enjoy it as a dip or a sandwich filling. It makes a wonderful addition to picnics or sack lunches.

> 1 package (8 ounces) tempeh, garden or seaweed variety
> 2 tablespoons Bragg Liquid Aminos or low-sodium soy sauce
> ¼ cup plain soy yogurt
> 1 tablespoon fresh dill, or 1 heaping teaspoon dried dill
> Pinch of cayenne
> 2 green onions, both green and white parts, finely chopped
> 2 tablespoons finely chopped celery
> 8 kalamata olives, pitted and chopped

❶ Cut the tempeh into ½-inch cubes. Steam it in a basket for 20 minutes, cool slightly, and put in a mixing bowl.

❷ In a separate small bowl, whisk together the liquid aminos or soy sauce, yogurt, dill, and cayenne.

❸ Mash the tempeh cubes while mixing in the yogurt dressing. They should begin to crumble and absorb the dressing.

❹ Add the green onions, celery, and olives. Chill before serving.

Serves 6. Per serving: 94 calories, 6 g fat, 7 g protein, 5 g carbohydrates, 2 g fiber, 116 mg sodium

---

Soups

Basil-Spiked Tomato Soup
Thai Chicken Soup
Czech Mushroom Soup
Black-Eyed Pea and Ham Soup
Shiitake Mushroom and Lentil Soup
"Cream" of Broccoli Soup
Black Bean Soup
Tofu Miso Soup
Gingered Carrot Soup
Chilled Avocado Soup
Vegetable Soup with Leeks
Winter Squash Soup with Thyme

← Gingered Carrot Soup, page 121, and Chilled Avocado Soup, page 122

Basil-Spiked Tomato Soup

From Merrilee Buckley, Cancer Lifeline intern

Quick and easy, this vibrant soup packs a super dose of tomatoes, a nutrition super food. For a fine meal, complement the dish with Honey-Glazed Green Beans with Almonds, page 131, and Roasted-Garlic Garlic Bread, page 152.

½ large yellow onion, finely diced
2 or 3 cloves garlic, minced (purée the onion and garlic in a food
    processor for a smoother texture)
2 tablespoons olive oil
3 tablespoons finely chopped fresh basil (2 tablespoons dried
    basil will work also)
Half of a 6-ounce can tomato paste
2 cups water
1 can (14½ ounces) tomato sauce
1 can (14½ ounces) diced low-sodium tomatoes
1 teaspoon salt
2 teaspoons freshly ground black pepper

❶ In a medium saucepan, sauté the onion and garlic in the olive oil for 3 to 5 minutes. Add the basil during the last minute of cooking time. Do not brown.

❷ Add the tomato paste. Cook for 1 minute.

❸ Add the water, tomato sauce, diced tomatoes, salt, and pepper. Cook until the soup simmers. Serve hot.

VARIATION:

Add low-fat milk or plain soymilk to the soup just before serving. Heat the milk before adding it and cook the soup, without boiling, for another 5 minutes.

Serves 4 (1-cup portions). Per serving: 85 calories, 0 g fat, 4 g protein, 20 g carbohydrates, 5 g fiber, 1,420 mg sodium

Nutrition Tip
*
In Mediterranean countries where people eat a lot of tomatoes and other fruits and vegetables, cancer rates are lower.

Thai Chicken Soup

From Chef Greg Atkinson

Coconut milk adds a subtle, creamy sweetness and the baby bok choy lends a tender crunch to this quick and savory soup.

4 cloves garlic
1 piece fresh ginger, 2 inches long
2 tablespoons vegetable oil
1 small onion, peeled and thinly sliced
1 medium red bell pepper, seeded and sliced
1 medium carrot, peeled and sliced
1 boneless chicken breast half, 6 ounces, thinly sliced
1 can (15 ounces) chicken stock
1 can (15 ounces) coconut milk
4 heads baby bok choy, sliced
A few leaves fresh cilantro
1 teaspoon crushed dried red chiles

❶ Rub the garlic and ginger through a very fine grater or put them in a blender with a couple of tablespoons of water and purée until smooth. Put the vegetable oil in a heavy-bottomed pot over medium-high heat and sauté the ginger and garlic for 1 minute, or until the aroma fills the air.

❷ Add the onion, bell pepper, and carrot to the pot and sauté for 1 minute longer. Add the chicken and cook for 5 minutes, turning the chicken pieces 3 or 4 times as they begin to brown.

❸ Pour in the chicken stock and coconut milk and bring the soup to a boil. Add the baby bok choy and cook for 2 minutes, or until the bok choy is tender. Transfer the soup to serving bowls and top with cilantro leaves and crushed dried red chiles. Serve at once.

Serves 4. Per serving: 268 calories, 10 g fat, 24 g protein, 28 g carbohydrates, 10 g fiber, 906 mg sodium

Czech Mushroom Soup

This healthy version of an old Czechoslovakian treasure preserves the creamy, rich taste.

1 cup chopped onion
½ cup chopped red bell pepper
4 cloves garlic, minced
¼ cup butter or non-trans fat margarine
1 cup sliced fresh button mushrooms
1 cup sliced fresh shiitake mushrooms
1 tablespoon low-sodium soy sauce
1 tablespoon chopped fresh dill
1 tablespoon sweet Hungarian paprika
2 cups low-sodium, nonfat chicken stock
¼ cup whole wheat pastry flour
1 cup nonfat milk or plain soymilk
1 cup low-fat sour cream
2 teaspoons fresh lemon juice

❶ In a medium saucepan, sauté the onion, red bell pepper, and garlic in 2 tablespoons of the butter or non-trans fat margarine until tender.

❷ Add the button and shiitake mushrooms, soy sauce, dill, paprika, and 1 cup of the stock. Cover and simmer for 20 minutes.

❸ Melt the remaining 2 tablespoons butter in a large soup pot. Whisk in the flour and cook for 3 minutes, stirring constantly. Slowly add the milk and the remaining cup of stock. Continue to stir over medium heat for another 10 minutes.

❹ Stir in the mushroom mixture. Cover and cook gently for 15 minutes.

❺ Blend in the sour cream and lemon juice and serve.

Serves 6. Per serving: 171 calories, 2 g fat, 6 g protein, 16 g carbohydrates, 2 g fiber, 188 mg sodium

Black-Eyed Pea and Ham Soup

Any type of bean may be used in this easy one-pot meal, but black-eyed peas lend a distinctive flavor. Accompany the soup with a side of Quick Corn Bread, page 150.

8 cups water if using dry black-eyed peas, 2 cups if using canned beans

1 cup dry black-eyed peas, or 1 can (15 ounces) any type of beans

2 cups low-sodium, low-fat chicken stock

12 ounces nitrate-free ham hocks (optional)

1 onion, chopped

2 stalks celery, chopped

2 cloves garlic, minced

½ teaspoon freshly ground black pepper

1 bunch fresh kale, collard greens, or other green leafy vegetable, chopped

1 strip dried kombu seaweed (optional)

> **Cooking Tips**
> *
> To reduce cooking time, substitute canned beans. If adding ham hocks, be sure to remove the bone and skin after cooking.

❶ If using dry black-eyed peas, bring 4 cups of the water to a boil and add the peas. Return to a boil, then remove the peas from the heat and drain. If using canned beans, omit this step and proceed with step 2.

❷ In a soup pot, combine the black-eyed peas with the remaining 4 cups water, or combine the canned beans with 2 cups water. Add the stock, the ham hocks if desired, and the onion, celery, garlic, and pepper and bring to a boil. Reduce the heat and simmer for 1½ hours. Add the greens and the kombu, if desired, and cook for another 30 minutes, or until tender.

Serves 4. Per serving: 389 calories, 14 g fat, 30 g protein, 36 g carbohydrates, 7 g fiber, 287 mg sodium

Shiitake Mushroom and Lentil Soup

From Margo Elbert, Cancer Lifeline intern

The earthy and rustic flavors of this wholesome soup are so satisfying, you can serve the dish as a main course.

2 tablespoons olive oil

1 large red onion, finely chopped

4 cloves garlic, minced

1 large stalk celery, chopped

1 pound fresh shiitake mushrooms, stems removed and caps coarsely chopped

1 cup chopped canned tomatoes with their juices

1 cup dried brown lentils, picked over and rinsed

5 cups vegetable stock (made from Vogue Instant Vege Base), or more if necessary

Chopped hijiki or arame (optional)

Salt or sea salt

½ cup chopped fresh parsley leaves

❶ Heat the oil in a heavy 4-quart saucepan over medium-high heat.

❷ Add the onion and garlic and cook, stirring, until it begins to soften, 2 to 3 minutes.

❸ Add the celery, stir, and then add the mushrooms. Continue cooking, stirring occasionally, until the vegetables soften and begin to release their liquid, about 5 minutes.

❹ Stir in the tomatoes, lentils, and stock. For extra flavor, add some chopped hijiki or arame. Bring to a boil.

❺ Reduce the heat to low, cover the saucepan, and simmer until the soup has thickened and the lentils are tender, about 1 hour. Add more stock if the soup is too thick.

❻ Season with salt to taste. Stir in the parsley and serve.

Serves 6. Per serving: 208 calories, 6 g fat, 13 g protein, 30 g carbohydrates, 12 g fiber, 899 mg sodium

"Cream" of Broccoli Soup

A delicious way to eat your green vegetables, this soup is easy to make, and any leftovers keep well in the refrigerator.

2 stems broccoli
4 cups low-sodium, nonfat chicken stock
2 tablespoons butter or non-trans fat margarine
½ medium onion, chopped
2 tablespoons whole wheat pastry flour
2 cups nonfat milk
4 ounces part-skim mozzarella, grated
1 teaspoon salt (may be omitted if chicken stock is salted)
½ teaspoon curry powder

❶ Cook the broccoli in the chicken stock for about 20 minutes, until tender. Remove the broccoli from the pan and reserve the liquid.

❷ Melt the butter or non-trans fat margarine in a medium skillet. Sauté the onion for about 5 minutes, until transparent. Add the flour. Stir until blended, then pour in the milk. Continue stirring until well heated and the mixture thickens slightly.

❸ Remove from the heat and thoroughly blend in the cheese, salt, and curry powder.

❹ Add the reserved cooking stock to the cheese sauce. Pour the soup in small batches into the food processor and blend slightly. Leave the broccoli coarsely chopped.

❺ If you need to reheat the soup before serving, be careful not to boil it.

Serves 6. Per recipe: 131 calories, 6 g fat, 11 g protein, 9 g carbohydrates, 2 g fiber, 586 mg sodium

Black Bean Soup

This tasty soup is packed with "super foods"—cruciferous cabbage family vegetables, beans, and shiitake mushrooms. A bonus is that preparation takes only about half an hour.

½ onion, chopped
2 cloves garlic, chopped
2 stalks celery, chopped
2 leaves kale or bok choy, finely chopped
2 fresh shiitake mushrooms, cut into small pieces
½ teaspoon ground cumin, or to taste
2 cans (15 ounces each) low-sodium chicken stock
2 cans (15 ounces each) low-sodium black beans
3 cups water
Plain low-fat yogurt
Chopped parsley

❶ Cook the onion, garlic, celery, kale, mushrooms, and cumin in 2 tablespoons of the chicken stock in a large nonstick skillet for about 10 minutes, or until soft.

❷ Add the remaining stock, beans, and water. Simmer for 20 minutes.

❸ Pour the soup into bowls and top each with a dollop of yogurt and some parsley.

Serves 6. Per serving: 226 calories, 2 g fat, 16 g protein, 38 g carbohydrates, 13 g fiber, 64 mg sodium

Tofu Miso Soup

A simple soup that combines the nutritious properties of tofu and sea vegetables with the rich flavor of miso.

3-inch strip dried kombu or wakame seaweed

3½ cups water

½ cup grated carrot

½ cup chopped bok choy or kale

¼ cup thinly sliced green onion, both green and white parts

½ cup cubed reduced-fat, silken, firm tofu

1 tablespoon brown miso

❶ Soak the dried seaweed in ½ cup water for 5 minutes. Drain, discarding the soaking liquid, and cut the seaweed into small pieces with scissors.

❷ Bring the remaining 3 cups water to a boil in a large pot. Add the seaweed and carrot and simmer for 5 minutes.

❸ Stir in the bok choy and cook over medium heat for 5 minutes. Add the green onion and tofu and simmer for 5 minutes.

❹ Remove from the heat and gently dissolve the miso into the soup. If you need to reheat the soup before serving, take care not to let it boil.

Serves 4. Per serving: 43 calories, 2 g fat, 3 g protein, 4 g carbohydrates, 1 g fiber, 186 mg sodium

Nutrition Tip
*

Miso is a paste made from grains and fermented soybeans. It comes in red, brown, or yellow varieties, depending upon the type of grain that has been added to the soybeans. This recipe calls for brown miso, which is made with barley.

Gingered Carrot Soup

From Herbs for Health, www.discoverherbs.com

The delicate play between the spice of the ginger and the sweetness of the carrots makes this soup a menu choice for all seasons. Serve it cold in the spring and summer and warm in the fall and winter.

1 pound carrots (about 6 medium carrots)
1 teaspoon minced fresh ginger
1 cup water
3 cups nonfat milk or plain soymilk
1 tablespoon olive oil
Salt and freshly ground black pepper

❶ Peel and slice the carrots. In a heavy saucepan, cook the carrots, ginger, and water over medium heat until the carrots are tender, about 10 minutes.

❷ Purée the soup in a blender. Add the milk, olive oil, and salt and pepper to taste, and whirl to mix. Serve hot, or chill and serve cold.

Serves 4. Per serving: 144 calories, 4 g fat, 7 g protein, 20 g carbohydrates, 2 g fiber, 135 mg sodium

Nutrition Tip
*
Like other deep orange vegetables, carrots contain antioxidants. Many studies have reported a relationship between low risk for cancer and high consumption of foods containing antioxidants.

Chilled Avocado Soup

Rich, creamy, and lightly spiced, this soup makes a meal when paired with a generous salad of mixed organic greens.

2 ripe avocados
1 cup soymilk or 2 percent milk
¼ cup cilantro leaves
2 tablespoons finely minced fresh ginger
2 tablespoons fresh lemon juice
½ teaspoon Asian chili sauce
1 teaspoon salt
½ cup plain low-fat yogurt
2 cups vegetable stock or nonfat, low-sodium chicken stock
½ cup finely chopped red bell pepper, for garnish

❶ Cut the avocados in half, discard the pits, and scoop out the flesh. Transfer to a food processor and purée until smooth.

❷ Add the soymilk, cilantro, ginger, lemon juice, chili sauce, and salt. Process until liquefied.

❸ With the machine running, pour the yogurt and stock through the feed tube.

❹ Transfer to a bowl and refrigerate until thoroughly chilled.

❺ Serve the soup in 4 chilled soup bowls. Place a little chopped red bell pepper in the center of each bowl. Serve at once.

Nutrition Tip
*
Avocados are a good source of monounsaturated fats.

Serves 4. Per serving: 221 calories, 18 g fat, 7 g protein, 15 g carbohydrates, 6 g fiber, 1,142 mg sodium

Vegetable Soup with Leeks

From Chef Jacques, Metropolitan Market, Seattle

This soup is served in many French homes during the winter months. The vegetables can vary with seasonal availability. Serve it with French bread.

2 large carrots
2 leeks
2 medium potatoes
2 medium turnips
1 sprig fresh thyme
10 cups cold water, or 5 cups low-sodium, nonfat chicken stock and 5 cups cold water
Salt and freshly ground black pepper

❶ Peel and wash the carrots, leeks, potatoes, and turnips. Cut into small pieces.

❷ Place the vegetables in a large cooking pot with the thyme. Add the water, bring to a boil, and simmer for 30 to 45 minutes, or until the vegetables are soft.

❸ Purée the soup in a food processor or food mill. Add salt and pepper to taste.

Serves 4. Per serving: 131 calories, 0 g fat, 3 g protein, 30 g carbohydrates, 5 g fiber, 96 mg sodium

Nutrition Tip
*
The leek, a member of the allium or lily family (and related to the onion), is also called the "poor man's asparagus."

Winter Squash Soup with Thyme

From Margo Elbert, Cancer Lifeline intern

Count on this colorful soup for a boost of important vitamins, minerals, and antioxidants.

2 teaspoons olive oil

1 large onion, finely chopped

2 carrots, peeled and finely chopped

2 stalks celery, trimmed and chopped

1 large sweet potato, peeled and cut into ½-inch cubes

1 butternut or hubbard squash, peeled, seeded, and cut into
   1-inch cubes

Leaves from 4 sprigs fresh thyme, or 1½ tablespoons dried thyme

4 to 5 cups vegetable stock (made from Vogue Instant Vege
   Base)

Salt and freshly ground black pepper

½ cup chopped fresh parsley leaves

❶ Heat the oil in a heavy 4-quart saucepan over medium-high heat. Add the onion, carrots, celery, and sweet potato and cook, stirring, until they begin to soften, 3 to 4 minutes.

❷ Add the squash, thyme, and stock, and season with salt to taste.

❸ Increase the heat to high and bring to a boil. Reduce the heat to medium-low, partially cover the saucepan, and simmer until the squash is tender when pierced with a sharp knife tip, about 20 minutes.

❹ Transfer the soup to a food processor or blender, or use an immersion blender, and process to the desired consistency.

❺ Return the soup to the saucepan and season with pepper to taste.

❻ Stir in the chopped parsley. Reheat before serving.

Serves 6. Per serving: 136 calories, 3 g fat, 4 g protein, 25 g carbohydrates, 5 g fiber, 421 mg sodium

---

Cooking Tip
✱
To save energy, cut the squash in half, seed, and place in a baking dish, flesh side down. Add water to cover the bottom of the dish, and cover. Bake in a 350°F oven for 25 to 30 minutes, until the squash is soft. Scoop out the flesh and add to the saucepan with the carrot/celery/sweet potato mixture.

Vegetables and Side Dishes

Yukon Gold Potato Salad
Snap Green Beans and Mushrooms with Piquant
   Dijon Vinaigrette
Honey-Glazed Green Beans with Almonds
Oven-Roasted Vegetables
Baked Sweet Potato Fries
Arame-Stuffed Mushroom Caps
Ruby Chard with Garlic, Chile, and Lemon
Garlic-Sautéed Greens
Grilled and Roasted Walla Walla Sweet Onions
   with Pine Nut Butter
Roasted Beets and Beet Greens with Marcona
   Almonds and Zolfini Beans
Stuffed Baked Potatoes with Nori
Broccoli with Sesame-Crusted Tofu
Sesame-Ginger Broccoli with
   Nori Rice
Quick Corn Bread
Roasted-Garlic Garlic Bread
Brown Rice
Millet
Quinoa
Buckwheat
Quinoa Pilaf with Toasted Sunflower Seeds
Polenta Squares
Spelt Pilaf with Baby Arugula
Spanish Rice
Tabouli

← Ruby Chard with Garlic, Chile, and Lemon, page 138, and Baked Sweet Potato Fries, page 135

Yukon Gold Potato Salad

From Chef Jim Watkins, Plenty Fine Foods, Seattle

A potato salad that not only is lightly dressed, but includes a medley of colorful vegetables. The addition of provolone cheese provides that special flavor.

Dijon Vinaigrette (recipe follows)
2 sprigs rosemary
2 pounds Yukon Gold potatoes
Salt and freshly ground black pepper
¼ cup olive oil
6 ounces low-fat Italian provolone, cut into bite-size chunks
2 medium zucchini, diced
5 Roma tomatoes, diced
1 yellow bell pepper, diced
1 green bell pepper, diced
1 bunch parsley, finely chopped
1 teaspoon celery seed

Dijon Vinaigrette

⅓ cup white wine vinegar
1 tablespoon Dijon mustard
1 teaspoon salt
1 teaspoon freshly ground black pepper
¼ cup olive oil

❶ For the vinaigrette, combine the vinegar, mustard, salt, and pepper in a blender. With the blender running, add the olive oil in a slow, steady stream and process until emulsified.

❷ For the salad, preheat the oven to 400°F.

❸ Strip the leaves from the rosemary sprigs and chop fine. Cut the potatoes into wedges and toss with the rosemary, salt and pepper to taste, and olive oil. Place in a baking pan and bake for 15 minutes. The potatoes should be tender but still firm enough for mixing.

❹ Toss the vinaigrette with the potatoes.

❺ Toss the cheese, zucchini, tomatoes, bell pepper, parsley, and celery seed with the potatoes until thoroughly combined. Serve in a large bowl or on a platter.

Serves 8. Per serving: 292 calories, 18 g fat, 8 g protein, 23 g carbohydrates, 2 g fiber, 511 mg sodium

---

Share your concerns, hopes, and joys with good friends who are fellow cancer patients or who have been touched by cancer.
—Clodagh Ash, cancer survivor

Snap Green Beans and Mushrooms with Piquant Dijon Vinaigrette

This slightly tart vinaigrette enhances the flavor of fresh vegetables. Serve with a loaf of crusty whole-grain bread.

> Piquant Dijon Vinaigrette (recipe follows)
> 1 pound fresh green beans
> 6 white mushrooms, thinly sliced
> 1 fresh tomato, sliced

Piquant Dijon Vinaigrette

> 1 clove garlic, finely chopped
> 2 shallots, finely chopped
> 3 tablespoons red wine vinegar
> 2 tablespoons olive oil
> 2 tablespoons water
> 1 tablespoon Dijon mustard
> Salt and freshly ground black pepper

❶ For the vinaigrette, mix the garlic, shallots, red wine vinegar, olive oil, water, and mustard in a small bowl. Add salt and pepper to taste.

❷ For the green beans, snap off the ends of the beans. Bring a large pot of salted water to a boil, and blanch the beans for 5 minutes (they should remain crisp). Chill the beans in cold water and drain.

❸ In a large bowl, toss the beans and mushrooms with the vinaigrette and garnish with the tomato slices.

Serves 4. Per serving: 121 calories, 7 g fat, 3 g protein, 13 g carbohydrates, 5 g fiber, 108 mg sodium

Honey-Glazed Green Beans with Almonds

From Merrilee Buckley, Cancer Lifeline intern

Crisp, slightly sweet green beans with a crunch of almonds make this recipe a winner.

    2 cups green beans, fresh or frozen
    1 tablespoon butter or non-trans fat margarine
    1 medium-size shallot, minced
    2 teaspoons honey or sugar
    2 tablespoons water
    ¼ cup sliced almonds

❶ Place the beans in a steamer basket in a saucepan and steam until tender.

❷ In a medium-size skillet over medium heat, melt the butter or non-trans fat margarine and add the shallot. Cook for 5 minutes, or until the shallot is translucent.

❸ Add the honey, water, and almonds and cook for 2 minutes.

❹ Add the steamed beans to the shallot-and-almond mixture and stir until coated. Serve hot.

Serves 4. Per serving: 110 calories, 7 g fat, 3 g protein, 10 g carbohydrates, 3 g fiber, 32 mg sodium

Oven-Roasted Vegetables

From Marianne Sakamoto, cancer survivor

Roasting vegetables heightens their flavor and works well for many types of vegetables. Vary the recipe according to the season. In winter, try root vegetables such as turnips and yams. In summer, add plum tomatoes, and in spring add cremini mushrooms.

 1 medium-sized green bell pepper
 1 medium-sized red bell pepper
 1 medium-sized yellow bell pepper
 3 small potatoes
 2 medium-sized carrots
 1 large onion
 2 or 3 cloves garlic
 2 to 3 tablespoons olive oil
 ¼ teaspoon each of assorted dried herbs: basil, oregano, thyme, rosemary (enough for a liberal dusting)
 Salt or sea salt and freshly ground black pepper

❶ Preheat the oven to 350°F.

❷ Seed the peppers and cut them into lengthwise strips.

❸ Cut the potatoes into fourths.

❹ Peel the carrots and cut them lengthwise into two pieces, and then into fourths if long.

❺ Peel the onion and cut into fourths.

❻ Chop the garlic.

→ *recipe continues*

❼ Put the vegetables in a large, resealable plastic bag and add the olive oil, herbs, and salt and pepper to taste. Seal the bag and shake to coat the vegetables with the olive/herb mixture.

❽ Remove the vegetables from the bag and spread on a cookie sheet.

❾ Bake, stirring every 20 minutes until the vegetables are browned on the edges and soft.

Serves 8. Per serving: 113 calories, 5 g fat, 2 g protein, 15 g carbohydrates, 3 g fiber, 11 mg sodium

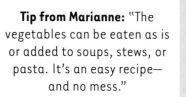

Tip from Marianne: "The vegetables can be eaten as is or added to soups, stews, or pasta. It's an easy recipe— and no mess."

Baked Sweet Potato Fries

From Merrilee Buckley, Cancer Lifeline intern

These potatoes are literally guilt-free. White potatoes may also be fixed this way, or try a combination of white and sweet potatoes.

> 2 medium-sized sweet potatoes or yams
> 2 teaspoons olive oil
> ½ teaspoon salt
> 1 teaspoon freshly ground black pepper
> 1 teaspoon garlic powder
> 1 tablespoon dried minced onion

❶ Preheat the oven to 375°F.

❷ Scrub the potatoes well. If using nonorganic potatoes, peel the skins. Slice each potato in half, then slice each half into 4 or 5 lengthwise pieces. They should resemble steak fries.

❸ Place the potatoes in a bowl and coat with the olive oil.

❹ In another small bowl, mix together the pepper, garlic powder, and dried minced onion. Add to the potatoes, making sure to distribute the seasonings well.

❺ Line a baking sheet with parchment paper or spray with nonstick cooking spray, and arrange the potatoes on the sheet.

❻ Bake for 25 to 30 minutes. Check for doneness at 20 minutes. Serve immediately.

Serves 4. Per serving: 120 calories, 2 g fat, 2 g protein, 23 g carbohydrates, 3 g fiber, 297 mg sodium

Arame-Stuffed Mushroom Caps

From the company chefs at Eden Foods

Arame is a mild-tasting sea vegetable that is pre-toasted so it cooks quickly. Pair the rich, meaty texture of this mushroom dish with a soup, such as Vegetable Soup with Leeks, page 123.

1 cup arame, rinsed and soaked in cold water for 5 minutes

2 cups water

18 portobello mushrooms

1 teaspoon light sesame oil

1 medium-sized onion, minced

¼ cup mirin

Juice of 1 lemon

2 teaspoons low-sodium soy sauce

Juice from 1 teaspoon grated fresh ginger (squeeze out the juice and discard the pulp)

¼ cup chopped fresh parsley, for garnish

❶ Preheat the oven to 350°F.

❷ Place the arame and water in a saucepan. Cover and cook over medium heat for 15 minutes. Remove the arame, rinse, drain, and mince. Stem the mushrooms, and place the mushroom caps in a 2-quart baking dish. Chop and reserve the mushroom stems.

❸ Heat the oil in a skillet and sauté the onion and mushroom stems for 3 to 5 minutes. Be careful not to overcook, as the mushrooms will shrink. Add the arame.

❹ Combine the mirin, lemon juice, soy sauce, and ginger juice. Pour half over the arame mixture and cook until the liquid evaporates. Stuff the mushroom caps with the arame mixture. Pour a little of the remaining marinade over each mushroom cap.

❺ Bake for 20 to 25 minutes. Remove from the oven, garnish with parsley, and serve.

Serves 6. Per serving: 71 calories, 1 g fat, 4 g protein, 15 g carbohydrates, 4 g fiber, 256 mg sodium

Nutrition Tip
*

Sea vegetables such as nori, kombu, hijiki, and wakame are an excellent source of calcium, magnesium, and potassium. They add minerals while enriching the flavor of foods. Information on ordering sea vegetables is available from Eden Foods, 888-424-EDEN, www.edenfoods.com; or Olean Harvest Sea Vegetables, www.ohsv.net.

Ruby Chard with Garlic, Chile, and Lemon

From Chef Tom Douglas, Dahlia Lounge, Palace Kitchen, and Etta's Seafood, Seattle

A brilliant vegetable, chard comes in a variety of hues, including green and rainbow (a mix of red, yellow, and green). Serve this lovely dish with Herb-Roasted Chicken, page 180.

3 bunches ruby or other chard (about 2 pounds, or 12 cups loosely packed, cleaned leaves)
¼ cup olive oil
¼ teaspoon dried red pepper flakes
2 teaspoons minced garlic
Kosher salt and freshly ground black pepper
4 lemon wedges

Chef's Tip
*
Use a large pan for cooking the chard, or cook it in batches. To make chard for more than 4 people, blanch it first in a pot of boiling water, shock it in ice water, and then squeeze all the water out. Reheat the chard by sautéing it in olive oil and garlic.

❶ Stem and wash the chard well. Shake off excess water.

❷ Heat the oil and red pepper flakes in a large sauté pan over medium-high heat, stirring occasionally, for 3 to 5 minutes.

❸ Add the chard and garlic and cook, stirring, for about 3 to 5 minutes. When the leaves are wilted, season to taste with salt and pepper and squeeze the lemon wedges over the chard.

❹ Divide the chard among 4 plates and serve immediately.

Serves 4. Per serving: 174 calories, 15 g fat, 4 g protein, 10 g carbohydrates, 4 g fiber, 484 mg sodium

Garlic-Sautéed Greens

Discover the exciting flavor of leafy greens. Mix and match a variety of seasonal greens for this quick sauté.

>1 tablespoon extra virgin olive oil
>8 cups sliced raw greens, such as kale, chard, collards, mustard
> greens, and broccoli rabe (1½-inch slices)
>3 green onions, both green and white parts, chopped (½ cup)
>2 large cloves garlic, chopped
>Salt and freshly ground black pepper

❶ Heat the oil in a large, heavy skillet over medium-high heat.

❷ Add the greens and green onions and keep them moving in the pan, turning frequently so that all the greens are heated.

❸ After 2 minutes, add the garlic. When the greens have turned bright green and begun to wilt, season with salt and pepper to taste. Continue to sauté a few minutes longer. Serve immediately.

Serves 4. Per serving: 107 calories, 4 g fat, 5 g protein,
15 g carbohydrates, 3 g fiber, 61 mg sodium

Phytochemicals called indoles give leafy greens such as kale, collards, mustard greens, and broccoli their "bite."

Grilled and Roasted Walla Walla Sweet Onions with Pine Nut Butter

From Chef Tom Douglas, Dahlia Lounge, Palace Kitchen, and Etta's Seafood, Seattle

Walla Walla onions are featured in this recipe, but you can substitute Vidalia, Maui, or Bermuda onions. Present the roasted onions on a bed of Ruby Chard with Garlic, Chile, and Lemon, page 138, or serve on Polenta Squares, page 158.

Pine Nut Butter (recipe follows)
4 Walla Walla onions
Olive oil

Pine Nut Butter

½ cup pine nuts (about 2½ ounces), toasted
3 tablespoons unsalted butter, softened
1 teaspoon grated lemon zest
½ teaspoon chopped fresh rosemary
¼ teaspoon freshly ground black pepper
¼ teaspoon kosher salt

Nutrition Tip
*
Chef Douglas uses 6 tablespoons of butter in this recipe, but reducing the amount to 3 tablespoons preserves the recipe's rich flavor and improves the recipe's nutrition profile.

❶ For the nut butter, chop half of the pine nuts. With a wooden spoon, mix together the whole and chopped pine nuts, butter, lemon zest, rosemary, pepper, and salt in a small bowl. Set aside.

❷ For the onions, fire up the grill and preheat the oven to 400°F. Peel the onions and cut them in half. Be careful to leave the root ends intact so the onions hold together. Brush the onion halves with olive oil and grill, cut side down, until lightly marked, about 3 minutes. Put the onion halves, cut side up, on a baking sheet, place in the oven, and roast until soft and cooked through, 30 to 40 minutes.

To sear the onions instead of grilling them, heat an ovenproof frying pan over medium-high heat with 2 tablespoons olive oil. Sear the cut sides until brown, about 3 minutes. Flip the onions and place in the oven to roast as directed.

❸ Remove the onions from the oven. Spread the cut halves liberally with the nut butter. Return to the oven to melt and bake in the butter, about 5 minutes.

Serves 4. Per serving: 260 calories, 21 g fat, 6 g protein, 16 g carbohydrates, 4 g fiber, 124 mg sodium

Chef's Tip
*
The nut butter can be made a few days ahead and stored, tightly wrapped, in the refrigerator or for a few weeks in the freezer. The onions can be grilled and roasted a few hours ahead and kept at room temperature. Return them to the oven to warm them through before spreading with the nut butter.

Roasted Beets and Beet Greens with Marcona Almonds and Zolfini Beans

From Chef Holly Smith, Cafe Juanita, Seattle

Warm, rich colors and flavors are combined in this winning recipe.

3 bunches baby beets with tops (if the tops are skimpy, add kale, ruby chard, or turnip greens)

¼ cup extra virgin olive oil, plus more for dressing beets

2 cloves garlic, minced

2 shallots, minced

¾ cup cooked zolfini beans (see the Chef's Note)

2 teaspoons chopped fresh marjoram

Kosher salt and freshly ground black pepper

Juice of ½ lemon

1 large red beet, roasted, peeled, and sliced into ⅛ to ¼ inch rounds (at room temperature for serving)

½ cup Marcona almonds, toasted

❶ Preheat the oven to 400°F.

❷ Remove the baby beets from their greens. Stem and wash the greens.

❸ Wash the beets and place in a roasting pan. Cover the beets halfway with water. Cover the pan with foil and roast the beets in the oven until tender, 20 to 30 minutes.

❹ Preferably with gloved hands to prevent staining, remove the outer skin from the warm beets after roasting them. Cut the beets into halves or quarters, depending on their size.

❺ In a large sauté pan, heat the olive oil over medium heat with the garlic and shallots. Let them sweat in the oil for 3 minutes, or until the garlic begins to turn slightly golden.

❻ Add the beet greens and zolfini beans to the pan.

❼ Add marjoram, salt, and finally the roasted baby beets. Toss to warm through. Add salt, pepper, and lemon juice to taste.

❽ Turn off the heat and keep the mixture warm in the pan.

❾ Dress the room-temperature roasted beet slices with a little extra virgin olive oil and a pinch of salt and pepper.

❿ Place a beet slice on each of 4 plates. Top each slice with some of the warm beet, beet green, and zolfini bean mixture.

⓫ Garnish with the Marcona almonds and, if desired, a final drizzle of best-quality extra virgin olive oil.

Serves 4. Per serving: 410 calories, 24 g fat, 15 g protein, 41 g carbohydrates, 15 g fiber, 629 mg sodium

Chef's Note
✳
Zolfini beans are grown in Tuscany. You may substitute cooked white beans, kidney beans, or garbanzos for the zolfini beans. Marcona almonds, grown in Spain, are considered to have more flavor due to higher fat content. Other varieties of almonds can be used.

Stuffed Baked Potatoes with Nori

From Margo Elbert, Cancer Lifeline intern

Baked potatoes take on a delectable new flavor with the addition of a sea vegetable. Nori is one of the richest sea-vegetable sources of protein.

> 6 medium-sized potatoes
> 6 small white onions
> 1 bulb garlic, tips sliced off
> ¼ cup white miso
> ¼ cup cold-pressed extra virgin olive oil
> 1 cup roasted nori, flakes or cut slivers (see the Cooking Tip)

❶ Preheat the oven to 350°F.

❷ Lightly oil a pie pan or roasting pan. Place the potatoes, onions, and garlic bulb (in their skins) in the pan to catch their juices.

❸ Bake for 45 minutes, or until tender. Set aside until cool enough to handle.

❹ Cut each potato in half and scoop the pulp out into a large mixing bowl, reserving the emptied shells. Remove the outer onion skins and cut the onions into small pieces, adding them to the potatoes. Squeeze the garlic cloves from their skins. Mix with the potato and onion.

❺ In a separate bowl, whisk together the miso and olive oil.

❻ Stir the miso–olive oil mixture and ½ cup of the roasted nori into the potato mixture. Mash together until blended.

❼ Spoon the filling into the potato half shells, making gentle mounds. Garnish with the remaining ½ cup roasted nori and serve.

Serves 6. Per serving: 334 calories, 10 g fat, 7 g protein, 56 g carbohydrates, 6 g fiber, 337 mg sodium

Cooking Tip
*

To cut nori, stack several sheets of nori (a standard sheet is 7 by 8 inches) and cut them together. With the short side toward you, cut with scissors along the long side. Make 8 equal strips, about 1 inch wide. Stack the strips and cut through them every $1/2$ inch, forming approximately $1/2$- by 1-inch pieces.

Broccoli with Sesame-Crusted Tofu

Tofu takes on the medley of flavors of this sesame-ginger marinade, and broccoli adds a generous serving of health-boosting greens.

Marinated Tofu (recipe follows)
4 stalks broccoli
1 red onion, sliced
1 red or yellow bell pepper, sliced thin
½ teaspoon sesame seeds

Marinated Tofu

3 cloves garlic, minced
½ cup balsamic vinegar
¼ cup low-sodium soy sauce
1 tablespoon toasted sesame oil
1 tablespoon grated fresh ginger
1 pound firm tofu, cut into ½-inch pieces

❶ For the marinated tofu, mix the garlic, balsamic vinegar, soy sauce, sesame oil, and grated ginger in a shallow bowl. Add the tofu and stir. Refrigerate for at least 30 minutes. If you prefer to serve this dish hot, heat the tofu in the microwave for 2 minutes.

❷ For the broccoli, trim and peel the broccoli stems and cut the broccoli into 2-inch pieces.

❸ Steam the broccoli florets and stems in a steamer basket until slightly crunchy, about 5 minutes. Let cool.

→ *recipe continues*

❹ In a medium bowl, toss the onion and pepper together with the broccoli.

❺ Add the tofu and sprinkle with the sesame seeds.

Serves 4. Per serving: 217 calories, 10 g fat, 15 g protein, 23 g carbohydrates, 7 g fiber, 658 mg sodium

---

Cooking Tip
✳
Make this a super-quick-cooking recipe by using packaged baked tofu instead of the marinated tofu. It is sold in a variety of flavors.

Sesame-Ginger Broccoli with Nori Rice

From Margo Elbert, Cancer Lifeline intern

> 6 cups cooked short-grain brown rice, cooled
> 3 tablespoons diced onion
> 4 stalks broccoli, steamed and chopped
> 1 tablespoon honey
> ¼ cup Bragg Liquid Aminos or low-sodium soy sauce
> 2 teaspoons toasted sesame oil
> 1 tablespoon grated fresh ginger
> 1 tablespoon sesame seeds, toasted
> 1 tablespoon rice vinegar
> 2 cups roasted nori, flakes or cut slivers (see the Cooking Tip on page 145)
> 1 cup chopped fresh parsley

In a large bowl, combine the cooked brown rice, onion, steamed broccoli, honey, Bragg Liquid Aminos, sesame oil, ginger, sesame seeds, rice vinegar, 1¾ cups of the nori, and ¾ cup of the parsley. Garnish with the remaining ¼ cup nori and ¼ cup parsley, and serve.

Serves 6. Per serving: 423 calories, 5 g fat, 15 g protein, 84 g carbohydrates, 8 g fiber, 674 mg sodium

Quick Corn Bread

From Margo Elbert, Cancer Lifeline intern

Quick and easy to make. Serve as an accompaniment to Grilled and Roasted Walla Walla Sweet Onions with Pine Nut Butter, page 140, or Three-Bean Vegetarian Chili, page 196.

¾ cup finely ground cornmeal

¼ cup polenta

½ teaspoon salt

1 tablespoon baking powder

½ teaspoon baking soda

¾ cup whole wheat flour

¼ cup unbleached white flour or soy flour

1 cup plain soymilk

2 tablespoons honey

2 tablespoons canola oil

1 cup drained canned corn kernels (reserve 2 tablespoons of the liquid)

❶ Preheat the oven to 350°F. Lightly oil a 9- by 5-inch or 11- by 3-inch loaf pan.

❷ In a large bowl, stir together the cornmeal, polenta, salt, baking powder, baking soda, and whole wheat and white flours.

❸ In another bowl, beat together the soymilk, honey, oil, and 2 tablespoons liquid drained from the corn.

❹ Add the wet ingredients to the dry, stirring just to mix, and then fold in the corn kernels.

❺ Scrape the batter into the prepared pan and bake until a knife inserted in the center comes out clean, 35 to 40 minutes.

❻ Remove from the oven and let cool on a rack.

❼ When completely cool, turn the bread out onto a cutting board or platter. Slice and serve.

Makes 1 loaf, 8 servings. Per serving: 193 calories, 5 g fat, 5 g protein, 33 g carbohydrates, 4 g fiber, 468 mg sodium

---

Roasted-Garlic Garlic Bread

From Margo Elbert, Cancer Lifeline intern

A crusty whole-grain bread infused with olive oil and garlic, this bread is the perfect accompaniment for any salad. Try pairing it with Spinach Salad with Poppy Seed Balsamic Vinaigrette, page 98.

Roasted Garlic (recipe follows)
¼ cup olive oil
¼ cup Worcestershire sauce
2 tablespoons low-sodium soy sauce or Bragg Liquid Aminos
2 tablespoons water
1 teaspoon dried dill
1 whole wheat sourdough French baguette

Roasted Garlic

5 bulbs garlic
About 2 tablespoons olive oil

❶ For the roasted garlic, preheat the oven to 350°F. Slice off the tips of the garlic bulbs and place them root ends down in a small baking dish. Drizzle the garlic with just enough olive oil to seep into the sleeves, and bake until the cloves are bubbling brown and bulging from roasting, about 40 minutes. Let cool.

❷ For the garlic bread, preheat the oven to 350°F. Combine the olive oil, Worcestershire sauce, soy sauce, water, and dill in a small saucepan over medium heat, and squeeze the roasted cloves into the mixture.

❸ Slice the French loaf lengthwise, and spread the garlic mixture evenly over the cut sides.

❹ Fit the loaf back together and slice it again crosswise, 1 inch thick. Wrap in foil and bake for about 30 minutes.

Serves 7. Serving size: 1-inch slice. Per serving: 230 calories, 8 g fat, 6 g protein, 35 g carbohydrates, 4 g fiber, 449 mg sodium

Cooking Whole Grains: Brown Rice, Millet, Quinoa, and Buckwheat

Whole grains contain a rich variety of vitamins, minerals, phytochemicals, and fiber. Processed grains like white flour or white rice lack the nutritional value of whole grains. Onion, garlic, or other chopped vegetables may be added to the grains before cooking. Seaweed, an excellent source of calcium, can also be added. (For dishes that cook longer than an hour, just cut the seaweed into small pieces and toss it in. For dishes that cook for less than an hour, soak the seaweed for 10 minutes until it is soft enough to cut, then cut it up and throw it in.) For consistent quality, consider using a rice cooker.

Brown Rice

2 cups water, or 1 cup low-sodium, nonfat chicken stock and 1 cup water
Pinch of sea salt
1 cup uncooked brown rice, short or long grain

For larger batches, use less water proportionately. For example:

5½ cups water (or 2 cups low-sodium, nonfat chicken stock and 3½ cups water)
3 cups uncooked brown rice

❶ Rinse the rice and let drain in a strainer.

❷ Bring salted water to a boil in a medium-sized pan. Add the rice and any chosen grains (see the Nutrition Tip), cover, and turn the heat down to a simmer. Cook undisturbed for 50 to 60 minutes.

Serves 4. Per serving: 171 calories, 1 g fat, 4 g protein, 36 g carbohydrates, 2 g fiber, 111 mg sodium

---

Millet

1 cup millet
3 cups water
Pinch of sea salt

❶ For a fluffier result, dry-roast the millet in a skillet by stirring it over medium heat until it smells toasty (optional).

❷ Bring the water to a boil in a medium saucepan. Add the millet and salt. Turn down the heat, cover, and simmer for 25 minutes.

Serves 2 to 3. Per serving: 378 calories, 4 g fat, 11 g protein, 73 g carbohydrates, 6 g fiber, 120 mg sodium

Quinoa

The name of this ancient grain is pronounced "keen-wah."

Pinch of sea salt
2¼ cups water
1 cup quinoa

Salt the water and bring it to a boil in a medium saucepan. Add the quinoa and turn down the heat. Cover and let simmer for 20 minutes.

Serves 2 to 3. Per serving: 318 calories, 5 g fat, 11 g protein, 59 g carbohydrates, 5 g fiber, 131 mg sodium

Nutrition Tip
✱

For more flavor and extra fiber, minerals, and protein, try adding other grains to plain boiled rice. Rye or wheat berries, dried corn, sweet brown rice, barley, lentils, kombu seaweed pieces, and wild rice all work well. Simply presoak ¼ cup of any selected grain for several hours, or bring the grain to a boil in a covered pan, simmer for 5 minutes, and set aside for an hour. Then add the grain to 1 cup of rice and boil as instructed.

Buckwheat

1 cup raw buckwheat groats (unroasted)
2 cups water
Pinch of sea salt

❶ Dry-roast the buckwheat in a skillet by stirring over medium heat until brown.

❷ Bring the water to a boil in a medium saucepan. Add the buckwheat and salt, turn down the heat, cover, and simmer for 20 minutes.

Serves 2 to 3. Per serving: 292 calories, 3 g fat, 11 g protein, 61 g carbohydrates, 9 g fiber, 8 mg sodium

Quinoa Pilaf with Toasted Sunflower Seeds

Quinoa is a nutty, sweet, quick-cooking grain that is high in protein.

1 cup quinoa
2¼ cups boiling water
Pinch of sea salt
1 tablespoon sautéed onion and/or toasted sunflower or sesame
    seeds

❶ Roast the quinoa in a skillet, stirring until golden. Add the quinoa and salt to the boiling water, cover, and simmer for 20 minutes.

❷ Stir in the onion and/or seeds.

Serves 4. Per serving: 160 calories, 2 g fat, 6 g protein, 30 g carbohydrates, 3 g fiber, 161 mg sodium

Nutrition Tip
*

Quinoa is a grain that comes from the Andes Mountains of South America. It was one of the three staple foods, along with corn and potatoes, of the Inca civilization. Quinoa was known then, and still is known in that area, as the mother grain.

Polenta Squares

Polenta can be a quick and satisfying meal when combined with cheese and served with vegetables, beans, or a salad. If refrigerated, polenta keeps for 3 to 5 days. To reheat, cut into squares and pop into the microwave. Top with your favorite tomato sauce.

2 cups low-sodium, nonfat chicken stock
1½ cups water
1¼ cups polenta (coarse cornmeal)

Optional Additions

¼ cup grated part-skim mozzarella, ricotta, or Parmesan cheese
1 fresh tomato, sliced
1 clove garlic, diced
½ teaspoon chopped fresh basil

❶ Pour the stock and water into a medium-sized saucepan.

❷ Add the polenta and bring to a boil, whisking constantly.

❸ Cook over medium heat, stirring frequently, for about 5 minutes, or until thick and smooth.

❹ Stir in the optional ingredients of your choice, and remove from the heat.

❺ Spread the mixture in a lightly oiled pan. Let stand for 20 minutes or until firm. Cut into squares.

Serves 4. Per serving: 205 calories, 3 g fat, 8 g protein, 36 g carbohydrates, 4 g fiber, 80 mg sodium

Cooking Tip
*

This corn porridge can be made on top of the stove in less than 15 minutes. The consistency may vary from dense and firm to soft and creamy. The texture softens with longer cooking. There are also good premade polentas that you can just slice, heat, and serve.

Spelt Pilaf with Baby Arugula

From Chef Charles Ramseyer, Ray's Boathouse Cafe, Seattle

Spelt is an ancient European grain that is a distant cousin to modern wheat. It has a hearty, nutty flavor that has been popular in Italy for centuries.

1 cup spelt (or substitute kamut or farro)
2 tablespoons olive oil
2 cloves garlic, minced
2 shallots, finely chopped
1 small carrot, peeled and finely chopped
1 stalk celery, finely chopped
1 small bulb fennel, finely chopped
½ cup sauvignon blanc
1 to 2 cups chicken or vegetable stock
2 cups packed baby arugula leaves, chopped
Kosher salt and freshly ground black pepper

> **Nutrition Tip**
> *
> Spelt, kamut, and farro are forms of wheat. Kamut is an ancient Egyptian wheat. Spelt is known as European wheat, while farro is Italian wheat. The three grains can be used interchangeably in recipes.

❶ Fill a 3-quart stockpot halfway with water (about 6 cups) and bring to a boil. Add the spelt and cook until al dente, about 20 minutes. Drain and set aside.

❷ Heat the oil in a 2-quart saucepan over medium heat. Add the garlic, shallots, carrot, celery, and fennel. Sauté until the vegetables begin to soften.

❸ Add the wine and cook until most of the liquid has evaporated. Add 1 cup of the stock and the cooked spelt. Simmer, adding more stock as necessary, until the spelt is slightly chewy and has the consistency of risotto, about 20 minutes.

❹ Remove from the heat and stir in the arugula.

❺ Season with salt and pepper to taste, and serve.

Serves 4. Per serving: 310 calories, 9 g fat, 8 g protein, 51 g carbohydrates, 3 g fiber, 922 mg sodium

Spanish Rice

From Jackie Patterson, cancer survivor

Color up your meal with this easy-to-prepare recipe that has excellent flavor.

1 cup uncooked long-grain brown rice
4 ounces turkey bacon
1 medium onion, chopped
1 small green bell pepper, chopped
1 can (15 ounces) stewed tomatoes
2 tablespoons butter or non-trans fat margarine
Salt or sea salt

❶ Preheat the oven to 350° F.

❷ Cook the rice, following the instructions on page 154.

❸ Chop the turkey bacon, and fry it in a skillet. Drain and remove it from the pan.

❹ Add the onion and pepper to the pan, and sauté until the onion is transparent.

❺ Drain the tomatoes, reserving the liquid; chop, and add to the pan.

❻ Mix the rice, turkey bacon, reserved liquid, sautéed onions, and tomatoes, and butter or non-trans fat margarine in a 2-quart casserole dish. Bake for 25 to 30 minutes, and serve.

Tip from Jackie: "I can cook once and eat four times by freezing single portions. I add steamed broccoli for my quota of leafy greens."

Serves 4. Per serving: 343 calories, 13 g fat, 10 g protein, 49 g carbohydrates, 5 g fiber, 773 mg sodium

Tabouli

Tabouli is a traditional Middle Eastern salad made from bulgur wheat—wheat that has been precooked, cracked, and dried. Since it needs no further cooking, it's quick to prepare and ideal for summer days.

1 cup reduced-fat chicken or vegetable stock
1 cup bulgur wheat (tabouli)
1 tablespoon olive oil
½ cup chopped fresh parsley
2 tablespoons chopped fresh mint, basil, or cilantro
3 tablespoons fresh lemon juice
2 cloves garlic, crushed or minced
1 large tomato, chopped
½ avocado, cut into ½-inch-thick slices
½ cucumber, diced (optional)
6 radishes, diced (optional)
Grated zest of 1 lemon (optional)

❶ In a medium-sized saucepan, bring the stock to a boil. Add the bulgur. Allow the stock to return to a boil, then cover and remove from the heat.

❷ When the liquid has been absorbed (about 15 minutes), fluff with a fork. Add olive oil, parsley, mint, lemon juice, garlic, and tomato.

❸ Refrigerate until cool.

❹ Garnish with sliced avocado or other options you choose.

Cooking Tip
✳
Use more garlic and fresh mint in the recipe to add more bite and a breezy taste.

Serves 3. Per serving: 281 calories, 10 g fat, 8 g protein, 44 g carbohydrates, 11 g fiber, 28 mg sodium

Entrées

Mushroom Asparagus Stir-Fry with Bay Scallops
Pan-Seared Petrale Sole with Lemon Caper Butter
    Sauce
Seafood Stew with Tomatoes and Saffron
Stovetop Fish Stew with Gingered Black Beans
Salmon with Sun-Dried Tomato Sauce
Steamed Red Rockfish on Winter Lentil Stew with
    Steamed Sunchokes
Pizza with Sun-Dried Tomato Sauce
Polenta Pizza
Potato Pancakes
Fajitas
Herb-Roasted Chicken
Citrus Marinade
Grilled Chicken Skewers with Tangerine-Ginger
    Glaze
Easy Vegetable Stir-Fry with Black Bean Sauce
Szechuan Chicken Stir-Fry
Broccoli and Lamb Stir-Fry with Soy-Sherry Sauce
Spicy Miso Peanut Noodles
Basmati Rice with Lentils
Sesame Tofu Squares with Greens over Grain
Three-Bean Vegetarian Chili
Zucchini and Tomato Gratin
Pronto White Bean Chili
Creamy Polenta and Bean Casserole
Turkey Meat Loaf
Cottage-Style Macaroni and Cheese
Shepherd's Pie

← Spicy Miso Peanut Noodles, page 191

Mushroom Asparagus Stir-Fry with Bay Scallops

Mushrooms are one of our Top 10 "Super Foods." This recipe showcases this versatile food with asparagus and bay scallops.

3 tablespoons low-sodium soy sauce

1 teaspoon cornstarch

2 tablespoons light sesame oil

6 asparagus spears, trimmed and cut into 1-inch pieces

6 mushrooms, sliced (either shiitake or button mushrooms)

3 green onions, both green and white parts, sliced (1 medium leek may be substituted, but use only the white and light green portions)

1 medium carrot, peeled and sliced

½ red bell pepper, cut into matchstick-size pieces

1 zucchini, sliced

3 large cloves garlic, finely chopped

2 teaspoons minced fresh ginger

8 ounces bay scallops, fresh or frozen, thawed if frozen

❶ Combine the soy sauce with the cornstarch in a small dish.

❷ Lightly coat a nonstick skillet or wok with the sesame oil. Turn the heat to high. Add the asparagus, mushrooms, onions, carrot, red bell pepper, zucchini, garlic, and ginger. Stir-fry for about 8 minutes.

❸ Add the scallops and cook for 6 minutes, or until the vegetables are tender and the scallops are white throughout.

❹ Stir in the soy sauce mixture and cook for 1 minute, or until thickened. Serve immediately.

Serves 4 to 6. Per serving: 128 calories, 6 g fat, 10 g protein, 9 g carbohydrates, 2 g fiber, 443 mg sodium

Pan-Seared Petrale Sole with Lemon Caper Butter Sauce

From Chef Kaspar Donier, Kaspar's Restaurant and Wine Bar, Seattle

> 3 tablespoons olive oil
> 4 fillets of petrale sole, 7 ounces each
> Kosher salt and freshly ground black pepper
> ¼ cup fresh lemon juice
> ¼ cup sauvignon blanc
> 1½ tablespoons capers
> 3 tablespoons cold unsalted butter, cut into thin slices
> 1 tablespoon chopped fresh parsley

❶ In a 12-inch nonstick sauté pan, heat the olive oil over medium-high heat.

❷ Season the sole fillets with salt and pepper.

❸ Place the fillets in the pan and sear until they begin to brown around the edges, 3 to 4 minutes. Turn and sear the other side for 1 minute.

❹ Carefully transfer the fillets to serving plates and keep warm.

❺ Combine the lemon juice, wine, and capers in the same sauté pan.

❻ Turn the heat up to high and cook until the sauce boils vigorously.

❼ Reduce the heat to medium-high and add the butter, stirring or shaking the pan continuously until all the butter has melted and it has emulsified into a smooth sauce.

❽ Stir in the parsley and season with salt and pepper to taste.

❾ Top the fillets with the sauce and serve immediately.

Serves 4. Per serving: 366 calories, 21 g fat, 38 g protein, 2 g carbohydrates, 0 g fiber, 440 mg sodium

---

Seafood Stew with Tomatoes and Saffron

Adapted from a recipe from Chef Greg Atkinson by Margo Elbert, Cancer Lifeline intern

Featuring a rich sauce of tomatoes, garlic, and kale, this hearty stew provides nutrition with flavor. Salmon fillets can be very successfully used in this recipe, but a white fish like halibut or snapper is more conventional. Add variety with shrimp, scallops, crab, or mussels.

2 medium onions, thinly sliced

¼ cup olive oil

2 tablespoon dried Greek oregano

½ teaspoon freshly ground black pepper

⅛ teaspoon cayenne (optional)

¼ cup mild red wine vinegar

3 cups vegetable stock (made from Vogue Instant Vege Base) or fish stock (made by boiling fish bones)

Generous pinch of saffron threads

2 tablespoons crushed garlic

1 can (22 ounces) crushed Italian-style tomatoes

2 pounds fish fillets or a combination of fish, shrimp, and scallops

1 large bunch kale, cut crosswise into fine ribbons (about 4 cups, packed)

❶ In a large, heavy saucepan over medium-high heat, sauté the onions in the olive oil until they just begin to brown. Stir in the oregano, pepper, and cayenne, if desired.

❷ Add the vinegar and let the mixture boil until the vinegar has evaporated somewhat and the onions are frying again.

→ *recipe continues*

❸ Stir in the stock, saffron, and garlic and bring the mixture to a boil. Add the tomatoes. (The stew can be made ahead of time to this point and kept refrigerated until 20 minutes before serving time.)

❹ Bring the stew to a boil. Add the fish fillets and kale.

❺ Reduce the heat to low and simmer for 15 minutes. Serve at once.

Serves 6. Per serving: 374 calories, 12 g fat, 46 g protein, 21 g carbohydrates, 4 g fiber, 1,003 mg sodium

Nutrition Tip
✳
Vary the hearty greens used in this stew. Try collards or mustard greens, or mix and match the greens. It's a great way to try new vegetables.

Stovetop Fish Stew with Gingered Black Beans

From Jeanne Ward, cancer survivor

This one-pot meal cooks in less than 15 minutes.

> 2 tablespoons olive oil
> 1 clove garlic, minced
> 1-inch piece fresh ginger, grated
> 1 medium onion, sliced
> 1 can (8 ounces) low-sodium stewed tomatoes
> 1 can (16 ounces) black beans
> 1 fish fillet, 14 ounces (halibut or choice of white fish)
> Salt or sea salt and freshly ground black pepper

❶ In a medium-sized skillet, heat the olive oil, add the garlic, ginger, and onion, and sauté until the onion is tender.

❷ Add the tomatoes and simmer for about 5 minutes.

❸ Add the black beans to the pan. Place the fish on top of the beans and tomato mixture, and simmer until it flakes easily. Add salt and pepper to taste.

❹ Serve the stew in bowls.

Serves 2. Per serving: 499 calories, 18 g fat, 34 g protein, 48 g carbohydrates, 16 g fiber, 1,130 mg sodium

---

Salmon with Sun-Dried Tomato Sauce

A variation on a Pacific Northwest favorite, inspired by the Greeks. This full-bodied, richly flavored tomato sauce complements a wide variety of dishes. Try the Pizza with Sun-Dried Tomato Sauce (page 174) made with this sauce, or use it on tofu or vegetables.

¼ cup Sun-Dried Tomato Sauce (recipe follows)
4 salmon fillets, 5 ounces each

❶ Heat a large nonstick frying pan over medium-high heat.

❷ Spoon the tomato sauce into the pan.

❸ Place the salmon on top of the sauce, skin side down.

❹ Cook for 5 to 7 minutes, or until brown. Turn the fish over and continue cooking for another 5 minutes, or until done.

Serves 4. Per serving: 269 calories, 16 g fat, 29 g protein, 1 g carbohydrates, 0 g fiber, 129 mg sodium

Sun-Dried Tomato Sauce

1 cup boiling water
1 cup sun-dried tomatoes
3 large cloves garlic
¼ cup fresh basil leaves
4 teaspoons fresh parsley leaves
1 tablespoon chopped shallot
1 tablespoon fresh lemon juice
1 tablespoon red wine vinegar
1 teaspoon Dijon mustard
1 teaspoon low-sodium soy sauce
2 tablespoons extra-light olive oil

¼ teaspoon salt

¼ teaspoon dried red pepper flakes

❶ In a medium bowl, pour the boiling water over the sun-dried tomatoes and garlic. Soak for 20 minutes.

❷ Place the basil, parsley, and shallot in a food processor and blend until very finely minced.

❸ Add the softened tomatoes and garlic and ½ cup of the soaking liquid. Blend thoroughly.

❹ Add the lemon juice, vinegar, mustard, soy sauce, olive oil, salt, and dried red pepper flakes. Blend until the sauce reaches a spreading consistency, adding extra soaking liquid if needed.

Makes 2 cups. Per tablespoon: 27 calories, 2 g fat, 1 g protein, 2 g carbohydrates, 0 g fiber, 126 mg sodium

Steamed Red Rockfish on Winter Lentil Stew with Steamed Sunchokes

From Chef Kaspar Donier, Kaspar's Restaurant and Wine Bar, Seattle

This elegant one-pot meal combines a rich array of flavors, colors, and textures.

1 tablespoon olive oil

½ cup chopped onion

6 cloves garlic, peeled and minced

½ cup diced red bell pepper

2 cups diced white cabbage

½ teaspoon caraway seeds

1 teaspoon Hungarian paprika

1 cup sherry

3 cups water

1 cup lentils

1 cup diced Roma tomatoes

1 teaspoon salt

1 pound sunchokes or Jerusalem artichokes

4 large leaves Swiss chard, coarsely chopped

4 red rockfish fillets, 3 ounces each, skinless and boneless

4 sprigs fresh herbs, for garnish

❶ Heat the olive oil in a 10- to 12-inch-wide sauté pan.

❷ Add the onion, garlic, pepper, cabbage, caraway seeds, and paprika to the pan and sauté until translucent, about 5 minutes.

❸ Add the sherry and water to the pan and stir to deglaze. Add the lentils, tomatoes, and salt. Mix well.

❹ Cover the pan with a lid and simmer for about 25 minutes.

❺ In the meantime, boil the sunchokes in a saucepan of salted water until tender, about 15 minutes, depending on their size. Keep warm.

❻ After the lentil stew has cooked for 25 minutes, add the Swiss chard and cook for 2 minutes more, until wilted.

❼ Place the fish fillets on top of the lentil stew.

❽ Cover the pot and steam the fish until cooked through and opaque, about 5 minutes.

❾ To serve, ladle some of the lentil stew in the center of each plate and place a fish fillet on top.

❿ Cut the sunchokes in half or quarters, and arrange around the fish.

⓫ Garnish each plate with an herb sprig.

Serves 4. Per serving: 499 calories, 18 g fat, 34 g protein, 48 g carbohydrates, 16 g fiber, 1,130 mg sodium

Pizza with Sun-Dried Tomato Sauce

A delightful Sunday night treat that's bursting with flavor. Olives, zucchini, onions, tomatoes, anchovies, capers, or hot peppers may be added to suit individual tastes. The crust recipe makes enough for two 12-inch pizzas.

Crust

1 cup lukewarm water or milk

1 package active dry yeast

2 cups unbleached all-purpose flour

½ cup whole wheat pastry flour

½ teaspoon salt

1 tablespoon olive oil

Cornmeal

Suggested Toppings

Olive oil

2 cups tomato purée

¼ cup Sun-Dried Tomato Sauce (page 170)

4 ounces part-skim mozzarella, grated

4 ounces part-skim ricotta cheese

8 cloves garlic, thinly sliced

Crushed dried red pepper

¼ teaspoon dried oregano

1 green bell pepper, sliced into thin rings

¼ pound mushrooms, thinly sliced

❶ For the crust, pour the lukewarm water into a medium-sized bowl and sprinkle in the yeast. Let stand 5 minutes, until foamy. In a small bowl, combine the all-purpose flour with the whole wheat pastry flour.

2 Add the salt, olive oil, and ½ cup of the combined flours. Beat for several minutes with a wooden spoon.

3 Add the remaining 1½ cups flour, ½ cup at a time, mixing by hand after each addition. The dough should be a bit softer than bread dough but not as sticky.

Cooking Tip
✳
The unrisen dough freezes well, so make extra for another meal or two.

4 Turn the dough out onto a surface lightly dusted with cornmeal and knead for 5 minutes. Clean and oil the mixing bowl, and return the dough to the bowl. Set in a warm place (an unheated oven works well) for 30 to 45 minutes, or until the dough has risen and doubled in bulk. Divide the dough in half and freeze it for later use (allow 3 hours to thaw), or proceed to step 5.

5 For the pizza, preheat the oven to 500°F.

6 Oil two 12-inch pizza pans.

7 Punch the dough down, return it to a cornmeal-dusted surface, and knead for several minutes.

8 Divide the dough in half and roll it out to fit the pans. Put it in the pans and press it into place. Brush the tops lightly with olive oil. Spread the tomato purée and sun-dried tomato sauce over the dough. Cover with the cheeses and toppings.

9 Bake the pizza on the top oven rack for 10 to 12 minutes, or until the crust is golden and the toppings are bubbling. Slice into wedges and serve immediately.

Per 12-inch pizza, 8 slices. Per slice (crust only): 257 calories, 7 g fat, 12 g protein, 40 g carbohydrates, 4 g fiber, 511 mg sodium

Polenta Pizza

An Italian dish that is easy to prepare yet achieves a sensational pizza-like result.

Crust

1 cup polenta (coarse cornmeal)
1½ cups low-sodium, low-fat chicken stock
1½ cups water
½ teaspoon salt
2 egg whites, beaten

Topping

½ cup diced onion
½ cup diced green bell pepper
½ cup diced red bell pepper
1 clove garlic, crushed
1 tablespoon olive oil
½ cup diced tomatoes
1 teaspoon dried oregano
1 cup grated part-skim mozzarella

❶ For the crust, combine the polenta, stock, water, and salt in a saucepan. Bring to a boil and simmer for about 10 minutes, stirring frequently until thick.

❷ Remove from the heat and blend in the egg whites.

❸ Spray a 9-inch pie pan with nonstick cooking spray. Form the polenta into a thick crust in the pan. Let stand.

❹ For the pizza, preheat the oven to 350°F.

❺ In a large skillet, sauté the onion, bell pepper, and garlic in the olive oil until tender. Remove from the heat and stir in the tomatoes and oregano.

❻ Spread the vegetable mixture onto the polenta crust. Cover with the grated cheese. Bake for 45 minutes. Cut into wedges and serve.

Serves 8. Per serving: 140 calories, 5 g fat, 8 g protein, 17 g carbohydrates, 2 g fiber, 239 mg sodium

Cooking Tip
✳
This pizza makes great leftovers for sack lunches.

Potato Pancakes

Recipes for potato pancakes vary only slightly, reflecting regional tastes. This variation includes leeks and garlic. Serve with applesauce or low-fat sour cream. Potato pancakes make a fine accompaniment for meat, poultry, or fish.

> 1 large russet potato, peeled and grated
> ½ cup chopped leek or onion
> 2 tablespoons all-purpose flour
> ¼ teaspoon salt
> ½ clove garlic, chopped
> 2 egg whites, beaten
> Olive oil

❶ Preheat the oven to 450°F.

❷ In a mixing bowl, stir together the potato, leek, flour, salt, and garlic.

❸ Fold in the egg whites.

❹ Dot a baking sheet with ½ teaspoon olive oil and drop a tablespoon of batter onto the oil. Repeat until all the batter has been used. Space the pancakes 1 inch apart.

❺ Bake for 15 minutes, or until golden brown. Turn the pancakes and cook for another 10 minutes. Serve right away.

Serves 3. Per serving: 84 calories, 1 g fat, 4 g protein, 15 g carbohydrates, 1 g fiber, 220 mg sodium

Fajitas

These tasty fajitas call for marinated flank steak, but you can substitute boneless, skinless chicken, fish fillets, or a 10-ounce package of silken, firm-style light or reduced-fat tofu. As another alternative, try half tofu and half beef, chicken, or fish. Serve fajitas with nonfat refried beans, rice, or Black Bean Salad, page 99.

1 (12-ounce) flank steak, cut into 1-inch strips and marinated in
    Citrus Marinade (page 181) for at least 30 minutes
1 medium onion, sliced
1 green bell pepper, sliced in long, narrow strips
1 red bell pepper, sliced in long, narrow strips
3 cloves garlic, diced
6 flour tortillas
2 tomatoes, chopped
Salsa (optional)
Minced cilantro (optional)
Chopped avocado (optional)
Plain nonfat yogurt or low-fat sour cream (optional)

❶ Heat a nonstick skillet or wok over medium-high heat. Remove the steak strips from the marinade, add to the skillet, and stir-fry for 5 to 8 minutes.

❷ Add the onion, green and red bell pepper, and garlic and stir-fry until just tender.

❸ Wrap tortillas in aluminum foil and heat in the oven for about 10 minutes. Fill each tortilla with an equal measure of meat and vegetables. Garnish with your choice of tomato, salsa, cilantro, avocado, and yogurt. Roll or fold the tortilla over the filling and serve.

Serves 6. Per serving: 308 calories, 9 g fat, 18 g protein, 39 g carbohydrates, 3 g fiber, 428 mg sodium

Herb-Roasted Chicken

This full-flavored chicken is easy to prepare and makes a wonderful meal paired with a flavorful vegetable, like Honey-Glazed Green Beans with Almonds, page 131, and Quinoa Pilaf with Toasted Sunflower Seeds, page 157.

1 whole frying or roasting chicken, 3 to 4 pounds
1 small onion, peeled and cut in half
2 cloves garlic
1 teaspoon poultry seasoning
1 teaspoon curry powder (optional)
½ cup water or chicken stock, plus more for basting

❶ Preheat the oven to 400°F.

❷ Remove the giblets and neck from the body cavity of the chicken. Rinse the chicken well and pat dry with a paper towel.

❸ Fill the cavity with the onion and garlic. Place the chicken breast side up in a roasting pan.

❹ Sprinkle the poultry seasoning and the curry powder, if desired, over the chicken and rub them in well.

❺ Add the water or chicken stock to the roasting pan.

❻ Cover the roasting pan and cook for 30 minutes. Baste with the pan drippings, adding more water or stock as necessary to keep the bird moist. Cook for another hour, basting as needed. Uncover the chicken for the last 15 minutes to brown the skin.

❼ Remove the skin before eating. The skin of a chicken contains a large amount of fat. Removing the skin reduces the total fat intake from 47 grams to 10 grams of fat per serving.

Serves 4 to 6. Per serving: 387 calories, 10 g fat, 68 g protein, 2 g carbohydrates, 0 g fiber, 246 mg sodium

Citrus Marinade

A sensational, semisweet marinade that includes garlic and citrus. It enhances the flavor of chicken, fish, lean meat, tofu, or vegetables.

⅓ cup fresh lime juice

1 tablespoon fresh lemon juice

⅓ cup low-sodium soy sauce

2 tablespoons Worcestershire sauce

1 tablespoon Grand Marnier (plum wine, sugar, or sherry may be substituted)

1 cup orange juice, preferably freshly squeezed

4 to 5 cloves garlic, pressed

½ cup chopped fresh cilantro

1-inch piece fresh ginger, grated (optional)

❶ Mix all ingredients together in a medium bowl.

❷ Set the meat or vegetables in a shallow dish and pour the marinade over it. Turn to coat all sides. Refrigerate for at least 2 hours.

❸ Remove the vegetables or meat from the dish and discard the marinade.

❹ Grill, broil, or stir-fry the marinated meat or vegetables.

Makes 2½ cups. Per recipe: 266 calories, 1 g fat, 9 g protein, 55 g carbohydrates, 1 g fiber, 3,446 mg sodium

Grilled Chicken Skewers with Tangerine-Ginger Glaze

From Chef Tom Douglas, Dahlia Lounge, Palace Kitchen, and Etta's Seafood, Seattle

These flavorful skewers can be enjoyed as an appetizer or as a main course with Brown Rice, page 154, and Garlic-Sautéed Greens, page 139.

Tangerine-Ginger Glaze (recipe follows)
4 boneless, skinless chicken breast halves
16 bamboo skewers, soaked in water for 30 minutes and drained
Peanut or vegetable oil
Kosher salt and freshly ground black pepper

Tangerine-Ginger Glaze

1 cup fresh tangerine juice
½ cup mirin
¼ cup soy sauce
2 tablespoons firmly packed brown sugar
1 tablespoon granulated sugar
2 teaspoons peeled and grated fresh ginger
½ teaspoon chopped garlic
½ teaspoon grated tangerine zest
1 teaspoon cornstarch
1 teaspoon water

❶ For the glaze, combine the tangerine juice, mirin, soy sauce, sugars, ginger, garlic, and zest in a small saucepan over medium heat. Simmer until reduced by half, about 10 minutes. Make a slurry by mixing the cornstarch with the water in a small bowl. Add the slurry to the simmering glaze and allow to simmer for another minute. The glaze should be as thick as maple syrup. Reserve one-fourth of the glaze in a separate small bowl.

→ *recipe continues*

❷ For the chicken skewers, fire up the grill or preheat the broiler. Cut each chicken breast into 4 pieces, about 2 inches by 1 inch each. Thread 1 piece of chicken on each skewer, brush with oil, and season with salt and pepper.

❸ Grill the chicken skewers over medium coals, or broil, turning them often and brushing 2 or 3 times with the glaze. Watch carefully, since the sugars in the glaze could burn; adjust the distance from the flame as necessary.

❹ When the chicken is cooked through, about 7 minutes, remove the skewers from the grill or broiler. Spoon the reserved glaze over the chicken just before serving.

Serves 4. Per serving: 306 calories, 5 g fat, 30 g protein, 27 g carbohydrates, 0 g fiber, 1,086 mg sodium

---

Chef's Tip
✱
The tangerine glaze can be made a few days ahead and stored in the refrigerator. When chilled, the glaze will firm up because of the cornstarch in it. To smooth out the glaze before brushing it on the skewers, warm it up and whisk it.

Easy Vegetable Stir-Fry with Black Bean Sauce

From Chef Jacques, Metropolitan Market, Seattle

A stir-fry with interesting flavors that can be varied with your choice of vegetables. Tofu can be added for extra protein. Serve with jasmine rice or Asian noodles.

1 tablespoon peanut oil
1 teaspoon chopped fresh ginger
1 teaspoon chopped garlic
1 (16-ounce) package of fresh stir-fry
    vegetables of your choice
1 tablespoon low-sodium soy sauce
1 tablespoon black bean sauce
1 teaspoon Asian chili sauce
¼ cup vegetable stock or water
1 teaspoon cornstarch
2 to 3 tablespoons water
1 teaspoon toasted sesame oil

> **Cooking Tip**
> *
> Keep a variety of prepackaged stir-fry vegetables in your freezer for quick, easy meal preparation.

❶ Heat the peanut oil in a wok or skillet over medium-high heat. Add the ginger and garlic and stir-fry for 30 seconds. Add the vegetables, soy sauce, black bean sauce, chili sauce, and vegetable stock. Stir-fry for 3 minutes.

❷ Mix the cornstarch with the water. Add to the stir-fry, along with the sesame oil. Give a final stir, and serve.

Serves 2. Per serving: 186 calories, 9 g fat, 6 g protein, 22 g carbohydrates, 7 g fiber, 759 mg sodium

Szechuan Chicken Stir-Fry

From Chef Jacques, Metropolitan Market, Seattle

Serve this spicy entrée with jasmine rice or Asian noodles. It's a quick dish to prepare.

4 skinless, boneless chicken breast halves, sliced into strips
3 tablespoons hoisin sauce
1 tablespoon low-sodium soy sauce
2 tablespoons minced garlic
2 tablespoons minced fresh ginger
2 tablespoons cornstarch
Szechuan Sauce (recipe follows)
1 tablespoon peanut oil
½ tablespoon Szechuan peppercorns, crushed
1 small zucchini, cut into strips 3 inches long by ¼ inch wide
8 ears canned baby corn
2 to 3 tablespoons water

Szechuan Sauce

¼ cup dry sherry
½ tablespoon Asian chili sauce
1 tablespoon sherry vinegar

❶ In a medium bowl, combine the chicken strips with the hoisin and soy sauces. Add 1 tablespoon each of the garlic, ginger, and cornstarch. Marinate for 20 minutes.

❷ For the Szechuan sauce, blend together the sherry, chili sauce, and sherry vinegar in a small bowl.

❸ Heat the peanut oil in a wok and stir-fry the chicken for 2 minutes. Remove the chicken and set aside.

❹ Stir-fry the remaining 1 tablespoon each of garlic and ginger with the Szechuan peppercorns for 20 seconds. Add the zucchini, corn, and Szechuan sauce. Cook for 2 minutes. Return the chicken to the wok. Mix the remaining tablespoon of cornstarch with the water and stir into sauce to thicken it.

Serves 4. Per serving: 239 calories, 7 g fat, 29 g protein, 12 g carbohydrates, 1 g fiber, 462 mg sodium

I arise in the morning torn between a desire to improve (or save) the world and a desire to enjoy (or savor) the world. This makes it hard to plan the day. —E. B. White.

Broccoli and Lamb Stir-Fry with Soy-Sherry Sauce

Serve with jasmine rice or Asian noodles.

Garlic-Ginger Marinade (recipe follows)
1 pound leg of lamb or loin meat, cut into thin strips
Soy-Sherry Sauce (recipe follows)
2 cups broccoli florets
2 tablespoons peanut oil
2 cloves garlic, minced
1 tablespoon cornstarch (optional)
2 to 3 tablespoons water (optional)

Garlic-Ginger Marinade

2 tablespoons oyster sauce
2 tablespoons low-sodium soy sauce
2 tablespoons cornstarch
1 tablespoon dry sherry
2 cloves garlic, minced
1 tablespoon minced fresh ginger

Soy-Sherry Sauce

¼ cup chicken stock
2 tablespoons low-sodium soy sauce
2 tablespoons sherry vinegar
1 teaspoon toasted sesame oil
1 teaspoon Asian chili sauce
1 tablespoon cilantro, minced

❶ For the marinade, in a large bowl, combine the oyster sauce, soy sauce, cornstarch, sherry, garlic, and ginger.

❷ Add the lamb to the marinade and refrigerate for 20 minutes.

❸ For the soy-sherry sauce, in a small bowl combine the stock, soy sauce, sherry vinegar, sesame oil, chili sauce, and cilantro. Set aside.

❹ Bring a medium pot of salted water to a boil, and blanch the broccoli in it for 2 minutes. Cool in cold water. Drain and set aside.

❺ Heat 1 tablespoon of the oil in a wok. Drain the lamb, add it to the wok, and stir-fry for 1 minute. Remove the lamb and set aside.

❻ Heat the remaining 1 tablespoon oil in the wok. Add the garlic and broccoli and stir-fry for 30 seconds. Return the lamb to the wok and pour in the soy-sherry sauce. Bring to a boil. If desired, mix the cornstarch with the water and stir it in to thicken the sauce.

Serves 4. Per serving: 352 calories, 24 g fat, 21 g protein, 12 g carbohydrates, 1 g fiber, 1,067 mg sodium

"I wish I could tell you what a good cry can do. I still have the same worries and concerns, but I feel 10 pounds lighter."

Spicy Miso Peanut Noodles

From Chef Seppo Ed Farrey, author of *3 Bowls: Vegetarian Recipes from an American Zen Buddhist Monastery*

Serve this fun noodle dish with Garlic-Sautéed Greens, page 139, on the side.

Peanut Sauce (recipe follows)

1 pound dried spaghetti or other noodles, such as buckwheat noodles

2 large carrots, peeled and coarsely grated

6 green onions, both green and white parts, thinly sliced

2 medium red bell peppers, cut into 1-inch slivers

3 tablespoons sesame seeds, toasted, for garnish (optional)

Peanut Sauce

¾ cup smooth peanut butter

½ cup white miso

¼ cup honey

2 tablespoons apple cider vinegar

1 tablespoon grated fresh ginger

2 cloves garlic, minced

½ teaspoon cayenne, or to taste

¾ cup hot water

❶ For the peanut sauce, in a medium bowl whisk together the peanut butter, miso, honey, vinegar, ginger, garlic, cayenne, and hot water until well combined and the mixture has taken on a glossy sheen.

→ *recipe continues*

❷ For the pasta, cook the spaghetti or other noodles in rapidly boiling water to the desired tenderness. Drain well. Rinse with cold water and drain again.

❸ Reserving a small amount of each vegetable for garnish, toss the carrots, green onions, and red bell peppers with the noodles and sauce. Garnish with the reserved vegetables and sesame seeds, if desired.

Serves 4 to 6. Per serving: 593 calories, 20 g fat, 21 g protein, 86 g carbohydrates, 6 g fiber, 788 mg sodium

---

Basmati Rice with Lentils

This is a quick and easy one-pot meal. Serve with a salad of baby greens and crusty whole-grain bread.

2 cups water
1½ cups low-sodium, nonfat chicken stock
1 small onion
2 cloves garlic, diced
2 carrots, peeled and sliced
¼ teaspoon ground white pepper
½ teaspoon ground cumin
½ cup uncooked basmati rice
½ cup lentils, washed

Cooking Tip
*
Peel onions under cold water. The water rinses away the volatile sulfur that causes teary eyes. Or freeze the onion for 20 minutes before chopping.

❶ In a large pan, combine the water, stock, onion, garlic, carrots, white pepper, and cumin. Bring to a boil.

❷ Slowly stir in the rice and lentils and return to a boil.

❸ Cover and reduce the heat to low. Cook for 45 minutes, or until the lentils and rice are tender.

Serves 2. Per serving: 420 calories, 3 g fat, 23 g protein, 80 g carbohydrates, 18 g fiber, 160 mg sodium

Sesame Tofu Squares with Greens over Grain

From Margo Elbert, Cancer Lifeline intern

Tofu, quinoa, amaranth, chard, spinach, and sesame seeds are rich sources of calcium. The nutrients in this fun-to-prepare dish offer support and protection for the body during times of transition and stress.

> 1 package (16 ounces) firm tofu, drained (or prebaked or seasoned tofu)
> 2 cups plus 3 tablespoons water
> 1 cup quinoa or amaranth, or a combination
> 1½ pounds greens, such as chard, spinach, or kale
> ¼ cup sesame seeds, toasted
> 2 tablespoons Bragg Liquid Aminos or low-sodium soy sauce, plus more to taste
> 2 tablespoons minced fresh ginger
> 2 tablespoons minced garlic

❶ Slice the tofu into bars and lay it over paper towels to "dehydrate" it, or drain off the moisture. You may have to do this several times until the tofu loses most of its moisture so that it will hold its texture and accept new flavors. Then cut the bars into cubes.

❷ Bring 2 cups of the water to a boil in a medium saucepan. Stir in the grains. Reduce the heat to low, cover, and cook until grain has absorbed the liquid and is tender, about 20 minutes.

❸ Chop the greens and place them in a steamer basket. In a 5-quart saucepan, bring an inch of water to a boil, and steam the greens just until they are wilted. Remove from the heat and set aside.

❹ Place the tofu cubes in a bowl with the sesame seeds and gently roll them around to coat them on all sides.

5 In a large, nonstick skillet, heat the remaining 3 tablespoons water and the Bragg Liquid Aminos. Add the minced ginger and garlic and sauté for 2 minutes.

6 Add the sesame-coated tofu cubes. Cook, turning occasionally, for 5 to 7 minutes.

7 Fluff the grain and spoon into 4 serving bowls. Place the greens over the grain and top with the tofu cubes. Serve with additional Bragg Liquid Aminos, if desired.

Serves 4. Per serving: 588 calories, 19 g fat, 36 g protein, 77 g carbohydrates, 13 g fiber, 696 mg sodium

Cooking tip from recipe tester Sara Snyder: "I used amaranth and kale for this. I also deviated from the recipe slightly by using some medium tofu, and I really liked the softer tofu. The softer texture sort of melted in your mouth. Also, I suggest adding a little fresh lemon juice. This recipe was great."

Three-Bean Vegetarian Chili

This hearty chili can also be served on a bed of rice, and Quick Corn Bread, page 150, makes a perfect accompaniment. For extra protein, cut firm tofu into $1/2$-inch cubes and add right before you add the chiles.

2 tablespoons olive oil
½ cup chopped onion
4 cloves garlic, minced
1 green bell pepper, diced
1 zucchini, diced
2 tablespoons chili powder
1 teaspoon ground cumin
1 teaspoon dried oregano
1 can (15 ounces) low-sodium pinto beans
1 can (15 ounces) low-sodium black beans
1 can (8 ounces) low-sodium garbanzo beans
1 can (15 ounces) tomato sauce
Hot chiles, chopped, to taste
Grated Cheddar cheese

❶ Heat the olive oil in a Dutch oven or saucepan. Add the onion, garlic, bell pepper, and zucchini and sauté for 5 minutes.

❷ Add the chili powder, cumin, oregano, beans, and tomato sauce. Simmer for 30 minutes to combine the flavors. Season with hot chiles to taste.

❸ Serve in bowls with a sprinkling of cheese.

Serves 6. Per serving: 338 calories, 7 g fat, 17 g protein, 55 g carbohydrates, 17 g fiber, 500 mg sodium

Zucchini and Tomato Gratin

From Chef Jacques, Metropolitan Market, Seattle

A delicious way to eat your vegetables.

1 tablespoon olive oil
2 cloves garlic, crushed
2 tablespoons chopped onion
2 sprigs basil, chopped
½ cup uncooked white rice
¾ cup water
2 small zucchini, sliced ¼ inch thick
4 medium tomatoes, sliced ½ inch thick
Salt and freshly ground black pepper
½ cup grated Asiago cheese, or ¼ cup grated Parmesan or
    Romano (these are sharper than Asiago, so using less still
    gives ample flavor)

❶ Preheat the oven to 375°F.

❷ Heat the olive oil in a gratin dish or ovenproof skillet. Sprinkle the garlic, onion, and basil on top of the oil. Add the rice and water.

❸ Layer the zucchini and tomato slices over the rice. Add salt and pepper to taste. Bake for 20 minutes.

❹ Preheat the broiler. Sprinkle the cheese over the top and broil until golden brown. Serve at once.

Serves 4. Per serving: 198 calories, 8 g fat, 7 g protein, 26 g carbohydrates, 2 g fiber, 50 mg sodium

Pronto White Bean Chili

A satisfying chili with a twist—it uses white beans instead of the usual kidney beans.

3 cups water
½ teaspoon chicken bouillon (dry powder or paste)
3 cloves garlic, chopped
1 medium onion, chopped
2 cups diced skinless chicken breast
1 can (7 ounces) chopped green chiles
2 teaspoons ground cumin
1 teaspoon dried oregano
¾ teaspoon cayenne
3 cans (15 ounces each) low-sodium white beans
¼ cup nonfat plain yogurt
¾ cup low-fat sour cream
1 cup grated reduced-fat Cheddar cheese
Chopped avocado (optional)
Chopped parsley (optional)

❶ Bring the water to a boil in a medium saucepan, and dissolve the bouillon in the boiling water.

❷ In a large pot, cook the garlic and onion in 2 tablespoons of the bouillon over medium heat until soft.

❸ Add the chicken along with another 2 tablespoons bouillon and cook until the chicken is white all the way through.

❹ Add the chiles, cumin, oregano, and cayenne, and then the beans and remaining bouillon. Mix well.

❺ Blend in the yogurt, sour cream, and cheese. Heat thoroughly, stirring to avoid sticking.

❻ Serve garnished with avocado and parsley, if desired.

Serves 6. Per serving: 422 calories, 12 g fat, 12 g protein, 49 g carbohydrates, 19 g fiber, 164 mg sodium

"It is amazing to be alive. That alone is worth celebrating every day and sharing with others."

Creamy Polenta and Bean Casserole

A satisfying meal that features a winning combination of fiber-rich plant protein, whole grains, and a flavoring of chicken. Serve with a vegetable dish such as Ruby Chard with Garlic, Chile, and Lemon, page 138, or a green salad such as Spinach Salad with Poppy Seed Balsamic Vinaigrette, page 98.

> 2 cups plus 2 tablespoons low-sodium chicken stock
>
> 1 cup polenta (coarse cornmeal)
>
> ⅓ cup grated part-skim mozzarella
>
> 1 whole chicken breast, skinned, boned, and cut into 1-inch cubes
>
> ½ cup chopped onion
>
> 2 cloves garlic, minced or pressed
>
> ½ teaspoon ground cumin
>
> ½ cup salsa
>
> 1 can (15 ounces) low-sodium beans, such as black, white, or kidney beans or black-eyed peas

❶ Preheat the oven to 350°F.

❷ Combine 2 cups of the stock and the polenta in a medium saucepan. Bring to a boil and cook, stirring constantly, until thick and smooth, about 5 minutes.

❸ Remove from the heat. Stir in the cheese and allow the polenta to cool.

❹ In a medium skillet over medium heat, cook the chicken in the remaining 2 tablespoons stock for about 10 minutes, or until chicken is white all the way through.

❺ Add the onion and garlic and cook until softened.

❻ Add the cumin and salsa.

❼ Rinse the beans in a colander to remove excess salt. Add to the chicken.

❽ Spread the cooled polenta in the bottom of a nonstick 9- by 13- by 2-inch baking dish.

❾ Spoon the chicken and beans over the polenta.

❿ Bake for 20 minutes, and serve.

Serves 4. Per serving: 356 calories, 5 g fat, 28 g protein, 49 g carbohydrates, 7 g fiber, 647 mg sodium

urkey Meat Loaf

A new twist on an all-American favorite. Substituting ground turkey for the traditional ground beef helps to significantly reduce the fat content. Steamed vegetables such as potatoes, carrots, turnips, or rutabagas make a fine accompaniment.

8 ounces ground turkey breast
8 ounces ground turkey (or substitute a 10-ounce package of tofu)
1 medium onion, chopped
2 cloves garlic, diced
1 medium carrot, peeled and coarsely grated
½ cup rolled oats, quick cooking or regular
2 eggs
1 can (7.5 ounces) low-sodium stewed tomatoes
⅛ teaspoon freshly ground black pepper (optional)

❶ Preheat the oven to 350°F.

❷ Mix the turkey (and tofu, if using) in a large bowl with the onion, garlic, carrot, oats, and eggs.

❸ Chop the tomatoes or purée them coarsely in a blender. Season with the pepper, if desired, and combine with the turkey mixture.

❹ Shape into a loaf and place in a 9- by 5-inch loaf pan.

❺ Cover the loaf with foil and bake for 60 minutes. Uncover and brown for about 15 minutes. Make sure the meat is well done.

❻ Let stand 10 minutes before serving. Cut into slices and serve.

Serves 6. Per serving: 219 calories, 9 g fat, 19 g protein, 15 g carbohydrates, 3 g fiber, 125 mg sodium

Cottage-Style Macaroni and Cheese

From Merrilee Buckley, Cancer Lifeline intern

Comfort food with a twist, this mac and cheese really delivers in the flavor department.

> 2 cups uncooked whole wheat elbow macaroni (about 4 cups cooked)
> 1 cup of 1 percent cottage cheese
> 1½ cups grated reduced-fat sharp or extra-sharp Cheddar cheese
> ½ cup low-fat milk
> ½ onion, puréed in a food processor or finely diced
> Salt and freshly ground black pepper

❶ Preheat the oven to 350°F.

❷ In a large saucepan, cook the macaroni according to the package directions. Drain and put in a mixing bowl.

❸ Add the cottage cheese, Cheddar cheese, milk, onion, and salt and pepper to taste. (For a smoother texture, purée the cottage cheese and milk together before adding them to the other ingredients.) Mix well.

❹ Place in a baking dish and bake for about 30 minutes, until the cheese is completely melted.

Serves 4. Per serving: 374 calories, 11 g fat, 27 g protein, 48 g carbohydrates, 5 g fiber, 251 mg sodium

---

Cooking Tip
*

You can add ¼ cup grated Parmesan cheese to this recipe for extra flavor.

Shepherd's Pie

From Margo Elbert, Cancer Lifeline intern

A traditional English favorite, this satisfying one-pot meal features flavorful vegetables from the cabbage family, a nutritional super food.

1½ pounds potatoes, peeled, quartered, and rinsed
¼ cup olive oil
Salt and freshly ground black pepper
2 cloves garlic, peeled and minced
1 medium onion, chopped
2 carrots, peeled and chopped
1 stalk celery, chopped
2 cups Brussels sprouts, quartered
¾ cup plus 3 tablespoons vegetable stock (made with Vogue Instant Vege Base)
1 tablespoon all-purpose flour
1 tablespoon chopped fresh thyme (or 1 teaspoon dried)
1 tablespoon chopped fresh rosemary (or 1 teaspoon dried)
Pinch of ground nutmeg

❶ Place the potatoes, 1 tablespoon of the olive oil, and salt and pepper in a large pot of cold water over medium heat.

❷ Bring to a boil and cook for about 15 minutes, until tender. Drain, reserving ½ cup of the cooking water.

❸ Mash the potatoes and add cooking water as needed, beating until fluffy with a hand mixer or wooden spoon.

❹ Preheat the oven to 400°F.

❺ Heat the remaining 3 tablespoons olive oil in a medium skillet over medium-low heat. Add the garlic, onion, carrots, celery, Brussels sprouts, and 3 tablespoons of the vegetable stock.

❻ Increase the heat to medium and cook for about 10 minutes, until evenly browned.

❼ Add the flour and cook, stirring, for 2 or 3 minutes more.

❽ Add the remaining ¾ cup vegetable stock, thyme, rosemary, nutmeg, and salt and pepper to taste.

❾ Reduce the heat to low and simmer, stirring occasionally, until thickened, about 5 minutes. Cool slightly, then transfer to a 9-inch pie plate or baking dish. Spread the mashed potatoes over the top, making peaks with the tines of a fork.

❿ Bake until the potatoes are browned and the dish is heated all the way through, 30 to 35 minutes. Let cool slightly, then serve directly from baking dish.

Cooking Tip
*
Experiment with other vegetables and combinations in this recipe. Try cauliflower, broccoli, green cabbage, or peas. Try adding mineral-rich sea vegetables such as nori, arame, or hijiki to the cooking vegetables.

Serves 6. Per serving: 236 calories, 10 g fat, 5 g protein, 35 g carbohydrates, 5 g fiber, 581 mg sodium

Desserts

Almond-Crusted Pears in Orange Sauce
Pecan Honey-Baked Apples
Raisin-Apple-Date Cookies
Chocolate Chip Cookies
Berry Fruit Crisp
Simply Delicious Berries
Date Treats
Baked Custard
Pumpkin Pie

← Baked Custard, page 217

Almond-Crusted Pears in Orange Sauce

A refreshing dessert that is easy to prepare, yet special enough for company.

1 tablespoon sugar
2 teaspoons fresh lemon juice
¼ cup fresh orange juice
1½ teaspoons cornstarch
1 teaspoon grated orange zest
1 pear, cored and sliced into 6 wedges
2 tablespoons chopped almonds

❶ In a small saucepan, combine the sugar, lemon juice, orange juice, cornstarch, and zest and cook over medium heat until thick, stirring constantly.

❷ Arrange the pear slices on serving plates. Pour the sauce over the pear slices. Sprinkle the chopped almonds on top and chill until ready to serve.

Serves 2. Per serving: 97 calories, 0 g fat, 1 g protein, 25 g carbohydrates, 2 g fiber, 1 mg sodium

Cooking Tip
*
To save your energy, buy nuts already chopped. Extra nuts can be stored in airtight containers in the refrigerator for 2 to 3 weeks and will keep almost indefinitely in the freezer.

Pecan Honey-Baked Apples

This dessert is a delicious way to get a serving of fruits, with a satisfying, protein-rich addition of pecans.

> 4 large baking apples
> ¼ cup chopped pecans
> ¼ cup raisins
> ¼ to ½ cup honey
> 2 teaspoons butter or non-trans fat margarine

❶ Preheat the oven to 375°F.

❷ Wash the apples and remove the cores to within ½ inch of the bottoms. Cut a strip of peel from around the top of each apple.

❸ Fill each apple with 1 tablespoon each pecans and raisins. Drizzle 1 to 2 tablespoons of honey over the nuts and raisins, and dab ½ teaspoon of butter or non-trans fat margarine on top.

❹ Place the apples in an 8- by 8-inch baking dish and pour ¾ cup boiling water into the dish. Bake for 40 to 60 minutes, until tender. Baste with the pan juices and serve.

Serves 4. Per serving: 257 calories, 7 g fat, 1 g protein, 53 g carbohydrates, 5 g fiber, 8 mg sodium

---

Raisin-Apple-Date Cookies

From Susan Hodges, author of *Healthy Snacks*

The sweetness of three rich fruits combines to make a cookie that tastes so good you won't miss the absence of added sugars.

1 cup raisins
½ cup chopped dates
1 cup peeled, sliced apple
1 cup apple juice concentrate
¼ cup butter or non-trans fat margarine, at room temperature
2 egg whites
1 teaspoon vanilla extract
2 cups whole wheat flour
1 teaspoon baking soda
1 cup rolled oats, regular or quick cooking
½ cup chopped walnuts

❶ Preheat the oven to 350°F.

❷ In a medium saucepan, combine the raisins, dates, apple slices, and apple juice concentrate. Bring to a boil over medium heat and cook for 10 minutes.

❸ Stir the butter or non-trans fat margarine into the hot mixture. Allow to cool.

❹ Pour the raisin mixture into a mixing bowl. Add the egg whites and vanilla. Beat well.

❺ Stir in the flour, baking soda, and oats. Add the walnuts.

❻ Drop by teaspoonfuls onto a parchment-lined baking sheet or a baking sheet sprayed with nonstick cooking spray.

❼ Bake for 15 minutes, until lightly browned.

Makes 48 cookies. Per cookie: 74 calories, 2 g fat, 2 g protein, 13 g carbohydrates, 1 g fiber, 40 mg sodium

---

"Sometimes what I need is just someone to listen, not necessarily to 'do' anything."

Berry Fruit Crisp

Bursting with the natural sweetness of berries, this summery dessert will become a favorite.

3 cups fresh or frozen berries (raspberries and marionberries are especially good)
⅔ cup unbleached all-purpose flour
2 tablespoons cornstarch
½ cup rolled oats, regular or quick cooking
½ cup nuts (such as pecans, walnuts, almonds, or hazelnuts), chopped
½ cup firmly packed brown sugar
1 teaspoon ground cinnamon
½ teaspoon salt
½ cup butter or non-trans fat margarine
Vanilla low-fat frozen yogurt

❶ Preheat the oven to 350°F.

❷ Place the berries in an 8-inch square baking pan.

❸ Combine the flour with the cornstarch, rolled oats, nuts, brown sugar, cinnamon, and salt in a mixing bowl. Work in the butter or non-trans fat margarine by hand until the consistency is crumbly. Sprinkle over the berries.

❹ Bake for 45 minutes, or until golden brown and bubbly. Serve warm, topped with frozen yogurt.

Serves 6. Per serving: 326 calories, 15 g fat, 6 g protein, 44 g carbohydrates, 4 g fiber, 230 mg sodium

Simply Delicious Berries

Savor the natural sweetness of strawberries in this elegant but simple recipe.

1 quart fresh strawberries
½ cup powdered sugar
1 cup nonfat yogurt

❶ Rinse and drain the strawberries in a colander. Arrange the berries on a serving plate.

❷ Set out bowls of powdered sugar and yogurt for dipping.

Serves 4. Per serving: 136 calories, 1 g fat, 4 g protein, 30 g carbohydrates, 2 g fiber, 48 mg sodium

---

Nutrition Tip
✳
Researchers have found that blueberries, strawberries, and raspberries contain chemicals found to protect against breast and cervical cancer.

Date Treats

From Sheila Taft, Cancer Lifeline horticultural therapist

Dates have been called nature's candy. Choose either fresh or dried dates that are glossy and plump. Avoid fruit with crystallized sugars on the surface.

> Dates (if using pitted dates, skip step 1)
> Walnut halves or whole almonds
> Shredded coconut or sugar (optional)

❶ Remove the pits from the dates.

❷ Push the walnuts or almonds into center of the dates.

❸ Sprinkle with shredded coconut or sugar, if desired. Store in a tightly covered container.

---

5 dates per serving. Per serving: 209 calories, 10 g fat, 3 g protein, 33 g carbohydrates, 5 g fiber, 3 mg sodium

---

Tip from Sheila: "These treats are great for a sweet tooth."

Chocolate Chip Cookies

These whole-grain cookies contain less fat and sugar than most cookies and make a nutritious snack.

½ cup butter or non-trans fat margarine
¼ cup date sugar
¼ cup firmly packed brown sugar
2 egg whites
½ teaspoon vanilla extract
¾ cup whole wheat pastry flour
¼ cup plus 2 tablespoons oat flour
½ teaspoon salt
½ teaspoon baking soda
½ cup nuts, chopped (walnuts or pecans are best)
½ cup chocolate chips

❶ Preheat the oven to 375°F.

❷ In a mixing bowl, blend the butter or non-trans fat margarine and date and brown sugars together until creamy. Beat in the egg whites and vanilla.

❸ In a separate bowl, sift together the whole wheat and oat flours, salt, and baking soda; then stir into the butter mixture.

❹ Stir in the nuts and chocolate chips.

❺ Drop the dough by teaspoonfuls onto a nonstick cookie sheet, spacing them well apart.

❻ Bake for about 10 minutes.

Makes 30 cookies. Per cookie: 71 calories, 4 g fat, 2 g protein, 9 g carbohydrates, 1 g fiber, 70 mg sodium

Baked Custard

A rich, smooth dessert to satisfy your sweet tooth.

2 cups low-fat (2 percent) milk
¼ to ⅓ cup honey
⅛ teaspoon salt
2 eggs
1 teaspoon vanilla extract
Ground nutmeg

❶ Preheat the oven to 325°F.

❷ In a medium saucepan, warm the milk with the honey and salt, stirring until the honey is dissolved.

❸ In a medium bowl, beat the eggs lightly, then slowly add the warmed milk, stirring constantly. Add the vanilla.

❹ Pour the mixture into 5 custard cups that have been placed in a baking pan. Sprinkle with nutmeg to taste. Pour hot water around the cups to a depth of 1 inch.

❺ Bake for 45 to 60 minutes. The custard is done when a knife blade inserted in the center comes out clean.

Serves 5. Per serving: 142 calories, 4 g fat, 6 g protein, 22 g carbohydrates, 0 g fiber, 126 mg sodium

Healing is more than just surviving. It is about living and thriving.

Pumpkin Pie

A full-flavored but low-fat version of a favorite recipe.

9 whole graham crackers
½ cup fruit juice
4 egg whites, lightly beaten
1 can (16 ounces) pumpkin
½ cup firmly packed brown sugar
¼ teaspoon salt
1 teaspoon ground cinnamon
½ teaspoon ground ginger
¼ teaspoon ground cloves
1 can (12 ounces) evaporated skim milk

❶ Preheat the oven to 425°F.

❷ Finely crush the graham crackers. Combine the crumbs with the fruit juice, just to moisten. Press into a 9-inch pie plate.

❸ In a large mixing bowl, combine the egg whites, pumpkin, brown sugar, salt, cinnamon, ginger, cloves, and evaporated milk. Blend until smooth.

❹ Pour the filling into the prepared pie crust.

❺ Bake for 15 minutes.

❻ Reduce the oven temperature to 350°F and bake for an additional 40 to 50 minutes, or until a knife inserted near the center comes out clean. Let cool before serving.

Serves 12. Per serving: 125 calories, 1 g fat, 4 g protein, 25 g carbohydrates, 1 g fiber, 254 mg sodium

References

Introduction

"The scientific evidence that diet and lifestyle are linked to cancer . . ." Byers, R., et al. (2002). American Cancer Society guidelines on nutrition and physical activity for cancer prevention: Reducing the risk of cancer with healthy food choices and physical activity. *CA: A Cancer J Clin*, 52 (2): 92–119.

"In fact, according to cancer experts, if people . . ." American Institute for Cancer Research(www.aicr.org). *Food, Nutrition and the Prevention of Cancer: A Global Perspective* (Washington, D.C.: American Institute for Cancer Research, 1997).

Top 10 "Super Foods"

Introduction

"Phytochemicals work in a number or ways . . ." Wattenberg, L.W. (1997). An overview of chemoprevention: current status and future prospects. *Proc Soc Exp Biol Med*, 216: 133–241.

Cruciferous Vegetables

"Researchers have found that people who eat more . . ." van Poppel, G. et al. (1999). Brassica vegetables and cancer prevention. Epidemiology and mechanisms, *Adv Exp Med*, 472: 159–68.

Beans

"Cancer researchers have determined that protease inhibitors . . ." Gould, M.N. (1997). Cancer chemoprevention and therapy by monoterpenes. *Environ Health Perspect*, 105: Supp 14: 977–79

"Phytic acid, another beneficial compound . . . " Fox, C.H., & Eberl, M. (2002). Phytic acid (IP6), novel broad spectrum anti-neoplastic agent: a systematic review. *Complement Ther Med*, 10(4): 229–34.

"The ancient Chinese considered soy . . ." Young, V.R. et al. (1984). Evaluation of the protein quality of an isolated soy protein in young men: Relative nitrogen requirements and effect of methionine supplementation. *Am J Clin Nutr*, 39(1): 16–24.

"Soy foods contain phytoestrogens . . ." Xu, X., et al. (2000). Soy consumption alters endogenous estrogen metabolism in postmenopausal women. *Cancer Epidemiol Biomarkers Prev*, 9(8): 781–86

"If you're a breast cancer survivor, you may . . ." Messina, M.J., & Loprinzi, C.L. (2001). Soy for breast cancer survivors: a critical review of the literature. *J Nutr*, 131 (11 Suppl): 3,095S–4,108S.

Berries and Cherries

"A variety of berries contain powerful antioxidant compounds called anthocyanins . . ." Halvorsen, B.L. et al. (2002). A systematic screening of total antioxidants in dietary plants. *J Nutr* 132: 461–91.

Onions, Garlic, Chives and other *Allium* Family Vegetables

"Allium vegetables also contain sulfur compounds called . . ." Milner, J.A. (2001). Mechanisms by which garlic and ally sulfur compounds suppress carcinogen bioactivation: Garlic and carcinogenesis. *Adv Exp Med Biol*, 492: 69–81.

Carotenoid-rich Foods

"A number of fruits and vegetables contain compounds called carotenoids . . ." Craig, W.J. (1997). Phytochemicals: guardians of our health. *J Am Diet Assoc*, 97(10 Suppl 2):S199–204.

Fish

"Fish is rich in omega-3 fatty acids, a . . ." Fernandez, E., et al. (1999). Fish consumption and cancer risk. *Am J Clin Nutr*, 70(1): 85–90.

"Fish seems to protect against cancer . . ." Reddy, B.S., et al. (1991). Effect of diets high in omega-3 and omega-6 fatty acids on initiation and postinitiation stages of colon carcinogenesis. *Cancer Res*, 51: 487–91.

Tomatoes

"Tomatoes contain lycopene . . ." Heber, D., & Lu, Q.Y. (2002). Overview of mechanisms of action of lycopene. *Exp Biol Med*, 227(10): 920–23.

"This phytonutrient also helps to restore . . ." Bertram, J.S. (1999). Carotenoids and gene regulation. *Nur Rev*, 57(6): 182–91.

"One study showed that when men ate . . ." Giovannucci, E., et al. (1995). Intake of carotenoids and retinol in relation to risk of prostate cancer. *J Natl Cancer Inst*, 87: 1,767–76.

Mushrooms

"Mushrooms have been revered in . . . ," "There is evidence that shiitake and maitake . . . ," and "Shiitake mushrooms contain forms of . . ." Ng, M.L., & Yap, A.T. (2002). Inhibition of human colon carcinoma development by lentinan from shiitake mushrooms *(Lentinus edodes)*. *J Altern Complement Med*, 8(5): 581–89

"Maitake mushrooms, also known as hen of . . ." Kodama, N., et al. (2002). Effects of D-Fraction, a Polysaccharide from *Grifola frondosa* on Tumor Growth Involve Activation of NK Cells. *Biol Pharm Bull*, 25(12): 1,647–50.

Nuts and Seeds

"Nuts appear to have a positive effect on . . ." Hebert, J.R., et al. (1998). Nutritional and socioeconomic factors in relation to prostate cancer mortality: a cross-national study. *J Natl Cancer Inst*, 90(21): 1,637–47.

"Walnuts have a compound called ellagic acid . . ." Narayanan, B.A., et al. (1999). p53/p21(WAF1/CIP1) expression and its possible role in G1 arrest and apoptosis in ellagic acid treated cancer cells. *Cancer Lett*, 136(2): 215–21.

"Flaxseed (30 grams a day) and a low-fat diet (20 percent fat) lowered . . ." American Institute for Cancer Research (www.aicr.org), *Nutrition After Cancer*, (Washington D.C., American Institute for Cancer Research, 2002) pp.20–26.

Green Tea

"Polyphenols in tea are known to inhibit . . ." Kazi, A., et al. (2002). Potential molecular targets of tea polyphenols in human tumor cells: significance in cancer prevention. *In Vivo*, 16(6): 397–403.

"One study found that Japanese . . ." Inoue, M., et al. (2001). Regular consumption of green tea and the risk of breast cancer recurrence: follow-up study from the Hospital-based Epidemiologic Research Program at Aichi Cancer Center (HERPACC). *Japan.Cancer Lett*, 167(2): 175–82.

"Researchers who studied the effect of green tea on prostate cancer . . ." Jatoi, A., et al. (2003). A Phase II trial of green tea in the treatment of patients with androgen independent metastatic prostate carcinoma. *Cancer*, 97: 1,442–46.

Nutrients That Promote Good Health

Macronutrients

Fat-Making the Best Choices

"The recommended intake of omega-3 fatty acids is 1.6 grams . . ." Trumbo, P., et al. (2002). Dietary Reference Intakes (DRIs) for Energy and the Macronutrients, Carbohydrate, Fiber, Fat, Fatty Acids, Cholesterol, Protein and Amino Acids. *J Am Diet Assoc*, 102(11): 1,621–30.

"There are 1.5 grams of omega-3 fats in six ounces of cooked . . ." Liebman, B. (September 1999). Do you know your vitamin ABC's? *Nutrition Action Healthletter*, www.cspinet.org/nah/ 9_99/vitamin_abc.htm.

Micronutrients

Vitamins-Necessary for Life and Growth

"Diets rich in foods containing . . ." Byers, T., et al. (2002). American Cancer Society 2001 Nutrition and Physical Activity Guidelines Advisory Committee. *CA Cancer J Clin*, 52: 92–119.

Minerals-The Body's Regulators

"Several studies have suggested . . ." Brooks, J.D., et al. (2001). Plasma selenium level before diagnosis and the risk of prostate cancer development. *J Urol*, 166(6): 2034–38.

Sea Vegetables-A Great Source of Minerals

"Sea vegetables contain 10 to 20 times . . ." Bradford, P., & Bradford, M. (1988). *Cooking with sea Vegetables*. Rochester, VT: Healing Arts Press. pp. 10–15.

Creating a Healthier Diet

Meat: Not the Center of the Plate

"In a primarily plant-based diet . . ." American Institute for Cancer Research. (1997). *Food, Nutrition and the Prevention of Cancer: A Global Perspective* (summary). (pp. 14–15). Washington, D.C: American Institute for Cancer Research.

Maintaining a Healthy Weight

How Much Fat?

"Here are some hints for maintaining a healthy weight . . ." Byers, T., et al. (2002). American Cancer Society Guidelines on Nutrition and Physical Activity for Cancer Prevention: Reducing the risk of cancer with healthy food choices and physical activity. *CA Cancer J Clin*, 52(2): 92–119.

Protecting Yourself Against Food-borne Illnesses

"The U.S. Department of Agriculture and the American Institute for Cancer Research . . ." For more information, visit www.aicr.org or www.usda.gov.

Preparing or Cooking

"Avoid eating sprouts . . ." U.S. Department of Health and Human Services, Food and Drug Administration. (July 9, 1999). Consumers Advised of Risks Associated with Raw Sprouts. www.cfsan.fda.gov/~lrd/hhssprts.html.

"Certain types of plastic . . ." Singleton, D.W., & Khan, S.A. (2003). Xenoestrogen exposure and mechanisms of endocrine disruption. *Front Biosci,* 8: S110–18.

"Wrap and refrigerate leftovers . . . " Birkett, D. et al. (November 2000). From Nutrition Action Health Letter Safe Food Quiz 2000. *Nutrition Action Healthletter* (Center for Science in the Public Interest), www.cspinet.org/nah/11_00/food_quiz2000.html.

Coping with Possible Side Effects of Cancer Treatment

Nausea

Ginger

"Ginger (*Zingiber officinalis*) is an herb recognized . . ." Duke, J. (1997). *The Green Pharmacy*. (p. 410). New York: St. Martin's Press.

Watermelon Popsicle recipe. Warren, J. (1992) *Super Snacks*. (p. 43). Torrence, CA: Frank Schaeffer Publications.

Sore Mouth or Throat

"Try Honey for a Sore Throat" Biswal, B.M., et al. (2003). Topical application of honey in the management of radiation mucositis. A Preliminary study. *Support Care Cancer* 11(4): 242–48.

Getting Organized

Organic Food: Is it Better?

"Twelve Fruits and Vegetables with the Most [and Least] Pesticide Residues." Environmental Working Group. (October 21, 2003). www.foodnews.org/reportcard.php..

Read Food Labels Before You Buy

"Use this rule of thumb . . ." Liebman, B. (1994). What's in a Label? *Nutrition Action Health Letter.*

Ideas for Quick-Fix Meals

American Dietetic Association. Vegetarian Nutrition Dietetic Practice Group. (2001). Quick Vegetarian Meals. Chicago, IL: American Dietetic Assoc.

American Institute for Cancer Research (www.aicr.org). (1994). Healthy Meals on Hand. Washington, D.C.: American Institute fir Cancer Research.

Warren, J. (1992). *Super Snacks*. Torrence, CA: Frank Schaeffer Publications.

Glossary

Allyl sulfides and diallyl disulfides (DADS): Sulfur-containing compounds found in vegetables of the onion family that act as cancer-blocking or cancer-suppressing agents.

Alpha-linolenic acid: Fatty acid of the omega-3 type.

Anthocyanins: Plant-based chemicals that give blue, blue-red, and purple colors to berries. These compounds act as antioxidants.

Antioxidants: Any of a variety of naturally occurring substances—such as vitamins A, E, and C; beta-carotene; and selenium—that can prevent or impede oxidation reactions.

Beta-glucan (D-fraction): Compounds found in maitake mushrooms that may stimulate the immune system and activate certain cells and proteins that attack cancer.

Carcinogens: Cancer-causing substances.

Carotenoids: A class of plant pigments found in dark green and orange vegetables and fruits that have proven antioxidant and immune-regulatory abilities.

Cruciferous vegetables: A group of vegetables (including cauliflower, cabbage, Brussels sprouts, broccoli, turnips, and rutabagas) containing substances that may protect against and fight cancer.

Detoxification enzymes: Liver enzymes that transform toxic molecules into water-soluble compounds that can be eliminated from the body.

Ellagic acid: A plant-based chemical found in walnuts that may slow cancer cell growth. Also beneficial in lowering high blood cholesterol levels.

Enzymes: Proteinlike substances formed in plant and animal cells that act as catalysts in initiating or speeding up specific chemical reactions. Usually destroyed by high temperatures.

Flavonoids: A group of plant pigments proven to protect against free-radical damage. They are noted for their antiinflammatory, antiviral, antiallergenic, and anticancer activities.

Free radicals: Highly reactive compounds with at least one unpaired electron, formed naturally within the body as a result of metabolic processes. The body is also exposed to free radicals as a result of sun exposure (radiation), smoking, drug and alcohol use, pollution, and stress. Free radicals can cause oxidative damage to cell membranes, tissue, and DNA, and contribute to aging and disease progression, including cancer.

Heterocyclic amines (HCA): Cancer-causing compounds formed when animal foods are barbecued, cooked on hot stones, fried, or broiled.

Hydrogenated fat: Polyunsaturated fats that have been chemically changed. These fats are widely used by the food industry in prepared foods, deep-fried foods, and shortenings. Like saturated fats, hydrogenated fats have a negative health impact.

Indoles: A group of compounds found in cruciferous vegetables that have exhibited anticancer activity.

Isoflavone: A group of compounds found in soy and other plant foods that may block the entry of estrogen into cells, reducing the risk of breast and ovarian cancer.

Lactose: A form of sugar found in milk and other dairy products.

Lactose intolerance: The inability to digest milk sugar (lactose) due to insufficient production of lactase, the enzyme that digests lactose. Lactase production typically declines with age and may be reduced by certain diseases and disease treatments that cause changes to the small intestine.

Legumes: The protein-rich seeds of plants such as kidney beans, soybeans, garden peas, lentils, black-eyed peas, and lima beans. Legumes are a good source of soluble fiber and can exert a stabilizing effect on blood sugar levels.

Lentinan: A form of complex sugar molecule in mushrooms that may stimulate the immune system and provide anticancer protection.

Lignan: Compounds found in flaxseeds that are transformed by the bacteria in our bodies into hormonelike substances (phytoestrogens) that may protect against tumor formation and growth.

Lycopene: A plant-based chemical found in tomatoes, watermelon, and other red and pink fruits and vegetables. Lycopene appears to reduce the risk of prostate and breast cancer.

Macronutrients: Protein, carbohydrates, and fats. They are called macronutrients because the body needs them in large quantities.

Macrophage: A type of white blood cell that filters the lymph system, engulfing foreign particles such as bacteria and cellular debris.

Micronutrients: Vitamins and minerals. They are called micronutrients because the body needs them in small quantities.

Monounsaturated fats: These fats, which are liquid at room temperature, come from plant sources that include olive, canola, avocado, and nuts and seeds—like pumpkin seeds, walnuts, and peanuts. They help to protect heart health.

Mucilage: A soft, moist, and viscous compound secreted by the seed covers of various plants, such as flax and slippery elm.

Nitrosamines: Carcinogens formed during digestion from nitrites—food additives used to prevent bacterial growth in processed meats such as hot dogs, bacon, ham, and sausage. In adequate doses, vitamin C can prevent the transformation of nitrites into nitrosamines.

Omega-3 polyunsaturated fatty acids: Fats found in cold-water fish, such as salmon, mackerel and herring, and in certain plants, nuts, and seeds, such as walnuts, flax seeds, and pumpkin seeds. Omega-3 fatty acids have been shown to positively affect immune responses, reduce the inflammation response to injury and infection, decrease the formation of blood clots, lower blood pressure, and reduce cholesterol.

Omega-6 polyunsaturated fats: Highly polyunsaturated fatty acids found primarily in animal proteins and vegetable oils. Modern diets are more abundant in this fatty acid than in omega-3 fatty acids.

Phytic acid: A phosphorous-containing compound found principally in the outer husks of cereal grains.

Phytochemicals: "Phyto-" means plant. "Phytochemicals" is a generalized term for a wide group of naturally occurring substances such as carotenoids that are found in plants and have been shown to have anticancer effects.

Phytoestrogens: Natural substances, found in soy and other plant foods, that exert estrogenlike effects. Compared to estrogen, phytoestrogen's activity is only 1:100,000. Because of this weak effect, phytoestrogens tend to counteract extreme estrogen levels. If estrogen levels are low, they will cause an increase in estrogen effect. If levels are too high, phytoestrogens will bind to estrogen-binding sites, thus decreasing estrogen's effects. In men, phytoestrogens seem to block testosterone, the hormone that can spur the growth of prostate tumors.

Phytosterols: Substances found in plants that may slow the production of cells in the large intestine and therefore slow tumor growth.

Polyphenols: An antioxidative group of phyto-chemicals.

Polysaccharide: A large and complex molecule made up of smaller sugar molecules.

Prostaglandins: Modified fatty acids that act in the body as messengers involved in reproduction and the inflammatory response to infection.

Protease inhibitors: Compounds that inhibit the action of protein-digesting enzymes and may retard the growth of human colon and breast cancer cells.

Polycyclic aromatic hydrocarbons (PAHs): Cancer-causing compounds formed when fat drips from grilled or broiled animal foods onto hot coals or stones. Smoke and flareups deposit these compounds on foods.

Polysaccharide: A form of highly complex car-bohydrates found in plants.

Psyllium: A soluble fiber that comes from a plant most commonly grown in India. Soluble fiber aids in intestinal health and regularity.

Saponin: A sugar compound with emulsifying properties. Saponins are thought to interfere with the process by which DNA replicates and may prevent cancer cells from multiplying.

Selenium: A trace mineral and important antioxi-dant that may help prevent cancer formation and pro-motion. Selenium functions either alone or as part of enzyme systems. Although selenium is needed only in small amounts, insufficient intake is common because of selenium-deficient soils. Low-selenium diets have been associated with an increased risk of cancer.

Sulphoraphane: A sulfur-based chemical found in plants that may stimulate enzymes in the body to destroy cancer-causing agents.

T-lymphocyte: A form of white blood cell that rec-ognizes and reacts to parasites, cancer cells, and cells infected by viruses.

Index

garbanzo beans
Hummus, 94
Three-Bean Vegetarian Chili, 196
garlic
Garlic-Ginger Marinade, 188–89
Garlic-Sautéed Greens, 139
health benefits/using, 6
Roasted Garlic, 152
Roasted-Garlic Garlic Bread, 152–53
ginger, 35
Garlic-Ginger Marinade, 188–89
Gingered Carrot Soup, 121
Ginger Tea, 35
Sesame-Ginger Broccoli with Nori Rice, 149
Stovetop Fish Stew with Gingered Black Beans, 169
Tangerine-Ginger Glaze, 183–84
grains
adding to rice, 155
cooking whole, 154–56
Great Grains Breakfast Cereal, 73
Sesame Tofu Squares with Greens over Grain,
194–95
Spelt Pilaf with Baby Arugula, 159
Tabouli, 161
green beans
Honey-Glazed Green Beans with Almonds, 131
Snap Green Beans and Mushrooms with Piquant
Dijon Vinaigrette, 130
greens
Garlic-Sautéed Greens, 139
Roasted Beets and Beet Greens with Marcona
Almonds and Zolfini Beans, 142–43
Sesame Tofu Squares with Greens over Grain,
194–95
green tea
health benefits/using, 12–13
grilled dishes
Grilled and Roasted Walla Walla Sweet Onions with
Pine Nut Butter, 140–41
Grilled Chicken Skewers with Tangerine-Ginger
Glaze, 183–84
grilling safely, 32
ham
Black-Eyed Pea and Ham Soup, 115

herbs
for diarrhea, 37, 38
Herb-Roasted Chicken, 180
Olive Oil and Herb Spread, 106
seasoning suggestions, 65–66
hetero-cyclic amines, 32
honey
Honey-Glazed Green Beans with Almonds, 131
Pecan Honey-Baked Apples, 209
for sore throat, 39, 40
Hummus, 94
immune system, possible dietary benefits for, 3, 6, 8–9
indoles, 2, 139
iron
boosting absorption of, 23
sources, 22
isoflavones, 4
Jerusalem artichokes. See sunchokes
kale
Garlic-Sautéed Greens, 139
in Seafood Stew with Tomatoes and Saffron, 167–68
Sesame Tofu Squares with Greens over Grain,
194–95
kamut, 159
labels, food, 56–58
lactose intolerance, 105
coping techniques, 40–41
lamb
Broccoli and Lamb Stir-Fry with Soy-Sherry Sauce,
188–89
laxatives, 37
leeks
Vegetable Soup with Leeks, 123
legumes, 17
health benefits/using, 3–5
serving size, 26
See also beans; peanuts
lemon
Citrus Marinade, 181
Pan-Seared Petrale Sole with Lemon Caper Butter
Sauce, 165
lentils
Basmati Rice with Lentils, 193
Shiitake Mushroom and Lentil Soup, 116–17
Steamed Red Rockfish on Winter Lentil Stew with
Steamed Sunchokes, 172–73

Salmon with Sun-Dried Tomato Sauce, 170–71
salsa
    Tropical Salsa, 95
salt, reducing in recipes, 64, 65
saponins, 3
sauce
    Lemon Caper Butter Sauce, 165
    Orange Sauce, 208
    Peanut Sauce, for 191–92
    Red Chili–Peanut Dipping Sauce, 93
    Soy-Sherry Sauce, 188–89
    Sun-Dried Tomato Sauce, 170–71
    Szechuan Sauce, 186
scallops
    Mushroom Asparagus Stir-Fry with Bay Scallops, 164
    in Seafood Stew with Tomatoes and Saffron, 167–68
scones
    Oat and Date Scones, 84–85
seafood
    Mushroom Asparagus Stir-Fry with Bay Scallops, 164
    Papaya, Shrimp, and Spinach Salad with Lime
        Vinaigrette, 96–97
    Ray's Café Seafood Margarita, 90–91
    Seafood Stew with Tomatoes and Saffron, 167–68
    See also fish
seasonings, 65–66
sea vegetables, 23, 137
    Arame-Stuffed Mushroom Caps, 136–37
    Sesame-Ginger Broccoli with Nori Rice, 149
    Stuffed Baked Potatoes with Nori, 144–45
seeds, health benefits/using, 10–11
    See also flaxseed
selenium, sources, 23
serving sizes, 25–28
Sesame Tofu Squares with Greens over Grain, 194–95
shake
    Yogurt Protein Shake, 72
    See also smoothies
Shepherd's Pie, 204–5
shopping, 55
    for healthy food, 60–61
    reading food labels, 56–58

shrimp
    Papaya, Shrimp, and Spinach Salad with Lime
        Vinaigrette, 96–97
    in Ray's Café Seafood Margarita, 90–91
    in Seafood Stew with Tomatoes and Saffron, 167–68
side dishes, 127–61
    Polenta Squares, 158
    Potato Pancakes, 178
    Quick Corn Bread, 150–51
    Quinoa Pilaf with Toasted Sunflower Seeds, 157
    Roasted-Garlic Garlic Bread, 152–53
    Spanish Rice, 160
    Spelt Pilaf with Baby Arugula, 159
    Tabouli, 161
    whole grains, 154–56
    See also vegetables
side effects, coping with, 33–45
    appetite loss, 41–42
    constipation, 36–37
    diarrhea, 37–38
    fatigue, 43–45
    lactose intolerance, 40–41
    nausea, 34–35
    sore mouth/throat, 38–40
    taste changes, 43
    vomiting, 35–36
    weight gain, 42–43
    weight loss, 42
smoothies, 70–71
snacks, quick, 62
soft foods, 38–39
sole
    Pan-Seared Petrale Sole with Lemon Caper Butter
        Sauce, 165
sore mouth/throat, coping techniques, 38–40
soup, 109–25
    Basil-Spiked Tomato Soup, 110–111
    Black Bean Soup, 119
    Black-Eyed Pea and Ham Soup, 115
    Chilled Avocado Soup, 122
    "Cream" of Broccoli Soup, 118
    Czech Mushroom Soup, 114
    Gingered Carrot Soup, 121
    Shiitake Mushroom and Lentil Soup, 116–17

Thai Chicken Soup, 112
Tofu Miso Soup, 120
Winter Squash Soup with Thyme, 124–25
soybeans, health benefits/using, 3–5
soymilk
Yogurt Protein Shake, 72
soy products
health benefits/using, 3–5
serving equivalents, 4
See also miso; soybeans; soymilk; tempeh; tofu
Soy-Sherry Sauce, 188–89
Spanish Rice, 160
spelt, 159
Spelt Pilaf with Baby Arugula, 159
Spicy Miso Peanut Noodles, 191–92
spinach
Papaya, Shrimp, and Spinach Salad with Lime
Vinaigrette, 96–97
Sesame Tofu Squares with Greens over Grain,
194–95
Spinach Salad with Poppy Seed Balsamic Vinaigrette,
98
spreads
Olive Oil and Herb Spread, 106
Tasty Tempeh Spread, 107
sprouts, avoiding, 32
squash
baked, 125
Winter Squash Soup with Thyme, 124–25
Zucchini and Tomato Gratin, 197
starchy foods, serving sizes, 27
stew
Seafood Stew with Tomatoes and Saffron, 167–68
Steamed Red Rockfish on Winter Lentil Stew with
Steamed Sunchokes, 172–73
Stovetop Fish Stew with Gingered Black Beans, 169
stir-fry
Broccoli and Lamb Stir-Fry with Soy-Sherry Sauce,
188–89
Easy Vegetable Stir-Fry with Black Bean Sauce, 185
Mushroom Asparagus Stir-Fry with Bay Scallops, 164
Szechuan Chicken Stir-Fry, 186–87
storing
food, 31
nuts, 208

strawberry
Strawberry Yogurt Protein Shake, 72
in Tropical Salsa, 95
Very Strawberry Smoothie, 71
substitutions
for fat reduction, 63–64
for sugar reduction, 64–65
sugar, reducing in recipes, 64–65
sulphoraphane, 2
sunchokes
Steamed Red Rockfish on Winter Lentil Stew with
Steamed Sunchokes, 172–73
Sun-Dried Tomato Sauce, 170–71
"Super Foods," xiv–13
supplements, 24
support for cancer patients, 46–49
sweet potato
Baked Sweet Potato Fries, 135
Szechuan Chicken Stir-Fry, 186–87
Szechuan Sauce, 186
Tabouli, 161
Tangerine-Ginger Glaze, Grilled Chicken Skewers with,
183–84
taste changes, coping techniques, 43
tea
Ginger Tea, 35
green, health benefits/using, 12–13
for nausea, 35
for sore mouth/throat, 40
tempeh
Tasty Tempeh Spread, 107
tofu
Broccoli with Sesame-Crusted Tofu, 146–48
Citrus Marinade, 181
Marinated Tofu, 146
Sesame Tofu Squares with Greens over Grain,
194–95
Tofu Miso Soup, 120
tomato(es)
Basil-Spiked Tomato Soup, 110–111
health benefits/using, 8–9
Pizza with Sun-Dried Tomato Sauce, 174–75
Salmon with Sun-Dried Tomato Sauce, 170–71
Seafood Stew with Tomatoes and Saffron, 167–68
Sun-Dried Tomato Sauce, 170–71

About the Authors

Kimberly Mathai, MS, RD, is a registered dietitian and licensed nutritionist. She is the nutrition educator at Cancer Lifeline, a non-profit support center for people with cancer and their caregivers. She has a private nutrition consulting practice with Nutrition by Design, in Seattle, WA. Ms. Mathai has written extensively on nutrition for medical textbooks, Internet-based companies, and popular magazines. She received her master's degree in nutrition from Bastyr University, in Seattle.

Ginny Smith is a freelance journalist who specializes in health subjects. Ms. Smith co-authored the first edition of *The Cancer Lifeline Cookbook* and co-edited *The CareWise Guide*.